The Brontës

by Peter Davies

GREENWICH EXCHANGE
LONDON

Greenwich Exchange, London

© Peter Davies 2000
All rights reserved

Student Guide to The Brontës

Printed and bound by Quorn Selective Repro Ltd, Loughborough
Tel: 01509 213456
Typesetting and design by Mike Rose and Albion Associates
Tel: 020 8852 4646

Greenwich Exchange Website: www.greenex.co.uk

ISBN 1-871551-24-2

CONTENTS

CHRONOLOGY

1812   The Rev Patrick Brontë marries Maria Branwell.

1814   Maria Brontë born.

1815   Elizabeth Brontë born.

1816   Charlotte born, 21st April.

1817   Branwell born, 26th June.

1818   Emily born, 30th July.

1820   Anne born, 17th January.

1820   April, the family settles at Haworth.

1821   Mrs Brontë ill with cancer. Her sister, Aunt Branwell, summoned to Haworth. April, Mrs Brontë dies.

1821-23 Patrick proposes to several potential successors. Is tartly rebuffed.

1824   Maria and Elizabeth go to Cowan Bridge School. They are followed by Charlotte and Emily.

1825   Maria and Elizabeth die in successive months. Charlotte and Emily brought home.

1825-31 The Brontë children brought up at Haworth parsonage.

1831   Charlotte to school at Roe Head.

1832   Summer. Charlotte back at Haworth to instruct her sisters.

1834   Branwell's portrait of his sisters.

1835   Charlotte goes to teach at Roe Head. Emily accompanies her as a pupil – and nearly dies from the experience.

1836   Charlotte sends her poems to Robert Southey.

1837   Branwell pesters the editor of *Blackwood's Magazine* and Wordsworth. Southey's patronising reply to Charlotte.

1840   Anne governess to the Robinsons at Thorp Green.

1842   February, Charlotte and Emily attend the Pensionnat
        Heger, Brussels. October, Aunt Branwell dies. They
        return home.

1843   Branwell joins Anne at Thorp Green as tutor to the
        Robinson children. Charlotte returns to Brussels. Falls in
        love with Heger. Returns home in humiliation.

1844   Charlotte's plan for a girls' school at Haworth comes to
        nothing. She writes impassioned love letters to Heger.

1845   June, Anne leaves Thorp Green, repelled by the family
        ethos. July, Branwell dismissed after affair with Mrs
        Robinson. Returns home to wallow in self-pity, drink and
        drugs. Charlotte alights on Emily's poems. Begins to
        think of a joint volume.

1846   May, the publication of *Poems* by Currer, Ellis and Acton
        Bell. Good reviews impart irresistible impetus to novel-
        writing.

1847   The Brontë *annus mirabilis*: October, *Jane Eyre,*
        November, *Wuthering Heights* and *Agnes Grey* published
        under their Bell pseudonyms. Branwell sliding inexorably
        into drink and drug addiction.

1848   June, *The Tenant of Wildfell Hall* published.
        24th September, Branwell dies. Emily stricken with
        tuberculosis from which, after only two months, she dies
        on 19th December.

1849   January, TB diagnosed in Anne. 28th May, she dies at
        Scarborough where she has gone on holiday with
        Charlotte.

1850   Charlotte, alone with her father, now, completes *Shirley.*
        October, *Shirley* published.

1852   Patrick Brontë's curate, Arthur Bell Nicholls, wooing Charlotte. Her father opposed, hoping for a grander match. December, she refuses Nicholls.

1853   January, *Villette* published.

1854   April, Charlotte accepts Nicholls, though with a somewhat tepid enthusiasm. June, Charlotte marries Nicholls. She becomes pregnant and suffers from life-threatening sickness.

1855   31st March, Charlotte dies.

1857   Charlotte's novel *The Professor,* written before *Jane Eyre* but rejected by her publisher, appears posthumously. Mrs Gaskell's biography of Charlotte published.

1861   Patrick Brontë dies.

1906   Arthur Bell Nicholls dies in Ireland, where he had returned after Patrick's death.

1 THE BRONTËS AND THEIR PUBLIC

WITHIN a very few years of the deaths of the Brontë sisters, the Brontë 'industry' as we know it today, had begun its work. Indeed, it can be seen to have been given its initial impetus by Mrs Gaskell's biography of Charlotte, which was published in 1857, only two years after Charlotte died. The book was a remarkable achievement and is still indispensable to an understanding of the ethos in which the Brontë sisters lived and worked. But it was also immediately 'controversial'. It had apparently traduced the character of Mrs Robinson, the married woman with whom Branwell Brontë had conducted an affair while tutoring her children, some years before. Under the threat of a libel suit from the lady (who had by then achieved respectability in a second marriage), the first edition had to be withdrawn and parts of it rewritten. Thus, the stage was set, from the very inauguration of Brontë studies, for an interest (frequently mounting to obsession) in the characters of individual members of the Brontë family which has ever since contended with – and often triumphed over – the desire calmly to estimate their literary merits.

Like Stratford upon Avon, Haworth, where the Brontës lived and worked, has become a place of pilgrimage for a host of enthusiasts, as if what remained today of this unattractive West Riding town could possibly yield any clue to the sources of that remarkable creativity. Over the past century and more, there has been an immense production of 'Brontëana' which extend their field of interest far outside the immediate members of the family, to include anyone who knew, or might have been known to them. This desire to dig for personal details has led to a frantic search for clues in their lives to account for the attitudes of their books, and vice versa.

Even if we grant that such exercises must always have a shred of legitimacy in them, in the Brontës' case they are almost always unhelpful. They have created a miasma of homage over their subject which only serves to obscure it. All that needs to be borne steadily in mind is that in the twenty-four months from May 1846, when their poems appeared, to May 1848 when Anne Brontë published *The Tenant of Wildfell Hall,* three, until then unknown, sisters impressed an ineradicable stamp on English literature. Though Charlotte continued to publish after her sisters' deaths, what she gave us in addition does not, I think, radically alter an assessment of the Brontë achievement.

Mrs Gaskell gave us what one might term the Romantic view of the Brontë lives: gloomy father, gaunt parsonage, religious dread, the sisters succumbing by inches to consumption. As such she has been accused of purveying the 'Charlotte version' of the Brontë story. There have been many attempts to prove this version tendentious, none more persuasive than that of Juliet Barker in her biography, *The Brontës,* of 1994. Barker set out to bury, once and for all, the Brontë myth by seeking to demonstrate that much of what we would regard as bleak, austere, uncomfortable, disease ridden and, above all, death accompanied was normality for such times as those, and is therefore scarcely worthy of remark.

On its appearance, her book was hailed as having revised the map of Brontë studies for good. Indeed, she is knowledgeable and compendious, and doubtless does well to make the attempt to demystify the subject. But for all its thousand pages, there is something important missing in such an account. Merely because people often died before their time, it does not follow that their survivors did not therefore grieve inconsolably. Sorrow and agony of mind, which in our culture have almost entirely been replaced with depression and other psychological disorders, are absent here. The impressive research work notwithstanding, we are left with a version of the Brontë story that is strangely lacking in imaginative sympathy with the passionate temper of that age.

2 PATRICK BRONTË

THE name Brontë is in itself a small stroke of genius. And any account of the life of the Brontë sisters has to begin with its 'onlie begetter', their father, the Rev Patrick Brontë. He was born Patrick Brunty (or Prunty) in 1777 in humble circumstances in Northern Ireland. As George Sampson has remarked: "A later Mr Shandy might amuse himself with speculating whether Charlotte Prunty would ever have achieved the fame of Charlotte Brontë, or whether Emily Brunty could ever have written *Wuthering Heights*."

In his passage from a two-roomed cabin in the rural parish of Ballyroney, County Down, via St John's College, Cambridge, to holy orders in the Church of England and, finally, to the perpetual curacy of Haworth, in Yorkshire, Brontë senior appears to have treated his family name with a certain creative licence. In Ireland the name appears as both 'Brunty' and 'Bruntee'. Contemporaries later remembered him there as 'Pat Prunty'. At Cambridge, where he went in 1802, he attempted to get himself registered as Patrick Bronte, perhaps influenced by the sonorous title of the Sicilian dukedom which had been bestowed on Nelson by a grateful Bourbon monarchy to thank him for driving the French out of Naples. Or the name may reflect the appeal to the would-be classical scholar of the equally sonorous Greek word for thunder.

Alas, this first attempt to distance himself from a name which (to English ears at any rate) spoke of plebeian origins was doomed to failure. Completely defeated by the vowel sounds of an impenetrable County Down accent, the St John's registrar gave up at the third attempt and inscribed the name 'Branty' in the college register. The would-be Bronte was determined. Returning to the register a couple of days later and seeing himself, according to his own notions of the thing, misspelt, Patrick had the register altered to 'Bronte'.

This might have been an end of the matter; but to the English eye (unlike the Italian) the terminal 'e' demands some sort of accent if the name is not to be thought of as monosyllabic. By the time the by-now ordained Patrick takes up his first cure at Wethersfield, Essex, in 1806, his surname has acquired an acute accent. At Dewsbury, three years later, we find him occasionally writing himself Brontě, the upvee imparting an inappropriately Slavonic ambience to the name. But by the time Patrick settles at Haworth, the last stop on his odyssey to respectability, the name has stabilised as Brontë. Doubtless Haworth's new perpetual curate felt that the diaeresis gave it an exotic quality which neither acute nor upvee does. In any event, Brontë it remained.

Patrick Brontë had graduated BA from Cambridge after a university career funded by the sizarship he had been awarded. He was ordained deacon at Fulham after graduating and took up a curacy at Wethersfield, Essex.

His first pastoral cure also provided him with his first experience of love. Mary Burder, his landlady's niece, was attracted by this loquacious young Irishman; he reciprocated by treating her in a somewhat cavalier fashion. Evidently marriage was not on his mind at that juncture. In any event, the end of their association seems to have been an acrimonious one. When, fourteen years later, as a widower with six children to support, he renewed his addresses to her by letter (at the same time tactlessly telling her that at her age she was not likely to have any better offers) she took great delight in giving him a decided refusal. We feel some sympathy with the undisguised *Schadenfreude* with which she recommends her impertinent (and now himself middle-aged) suitor and his "small but sweet family" to the good graces of a beneficent Providence.

When he eventually came to marry Patrick did, however, make an excellent choice. By 1812 he was installed in a curacy at Hartshead, not far from Dewsbury in the West Riding of Yorkshire. There he met Maria Branwell, one of five daughters of a Penzance merchant, who was helping out a married cousin with the management of her husband's Wesleyan school. More important to literary history, she was, as her letters give evidence, a woman of education, sensibility and spirit. A courtship between her and Hartshead's new curate ripened fast. When he asked her to marry him she agreed without hesitation to the permanent exchange of the Cornish Riviera's subtropical climate and the winsome panorama of Mount's Bay and St Michael's Mount for the rigours of Pennine Yorkshire and the grim backdrop of the scenery of industrial revolution.

They were married in December 1812 and set up home at Hartshead. There, their first child, Maria, was born in April 1814 and their second, Elizabeth, on 8th February 1815. Shortly afterwards, Patrick was translated to the perpetual curacy of Thornton, near Bradford, where his remaining children were born: Charlotte on 21st April 1816; Branwell on 26th June 1817; Emily on 30th July 1818; Anne on 17th January 1820.

In April 1820 the Brontë family moved to Haworth, a few miles above Keighley on the River Worth. The Rev Patrick Brontë had some months before been appointed perpetual curate, there. Even before Brontë took up his curacy, Haworth was already celebrated throughout a part of the West Riding where the barriers between Methodism and Evangelical Anglicanism were not strongly maintained. John and Charles Wesley had preached there to packed houses. The name of Charles Grimshaw, one of Patrick's 18th century predecessors, still resounded throughout the neighbourhood. In his day Grimshaw had been virtually number three in the Methodist hierarchy and his name was a byword for muscular Christianity which could frighten even the dour, self sufficient men of the West Riding into his church on pain of fire and brimstone. Yet it was to be for a successor from County Down to become the most celebrated of all Haworth's incumbents.

By the time the Brontës made their move to Haworth, Patrick's wife was already gravely ill with the cancer which was to end her life in the following year. Early in 1821 Aunt Branwell had been summoned from Penzance to tend her sister. Thus, by the time Maria Brontë died on 15th September 1821 the key elements of what was to become the most famous literary family of all time, were in place: the by now some what chastened and brooding Anglican parson; his proselytising Cornish Methodist sister-in-law; six precocious children;

and a gloomy, draughty parsonage set on the verge of a wild expanse of Pennine moor.

In a centrally-heated, double-glazed age like ours, it takes a resolute leap of the imagination to envisage what life was like in the hills of the West Riding of Yorkshire in the 1820s. The area, abutting, as it does, neighbouring Lancashire is a resolutely chill and wet one. The prevailing Westerly winds coming in off the Irish Sea drive an airstream which rises and cools as it climbs over the upland Lancashire forests of Pendle and Trawden, depositing rain in abundance on them and on the adjacent Yorkshire moors of Haworth and Keighley.

Quite apart from whatever personal austerities Patrick Brontë may have practised as a house manager, the daily existence of children in those days was a matter of often freezing cold, damp, draughty houses, whose ill-fitting windows gave little protection against the fury of the elements. Rising on winter mornings to try to complete basic ablutions against the competing claims of a large number of siblings was an ordeal. Venturing abroad, whether down the hill into Haworth village or up onto the moors was more likely than not to end in shoes sodden through, cold, wet feet, frozen fingers and clothes saturated to the skin. Sanitation as we know it was unknown. Disease was a constant companion. Infant mortality was high. In Haworth it was shocking even by the grim standards of the time. Forty per cent of all children died before the age of five. The baneful presence of that dread triumvirate, tuberculosis, cholera and typhus apart, daily life, even in a moderately well-regulated household such as the parsonage, was for small children a ceaseless cycle of raw sore throats, streaming colds, racking coughs, bronchial infections, ulcerated mouths, chapped hands and the agony of chilblains.

Anyone who visits Haworth today (little though it can resemble its grimmer self of former times) can see that far from giving the effect of being perched on glorious moors, it is a place of singularly hard-favoured aspect which the trappings of modern culture tourism seem to accentuate rather than diminish. The character of the men of the West Riding is of a piece with the terrain they inhabit: cross-grained, close-fisted and resolute. In her *Life of Charlotte Brontë* Mrs Gaskell recounts a story which wonderfully illustrates the psychology of the type.

> A man that she [Charlotte Brontë] knew, who was a small manufacturer, had engaged in many local speculations, which had always turned out well, and thereby rendered him a person of some wealth. He was rather past middle age when he bethought him of insuring his life; and he had only just taken out his policy when he fell ill of an acute disease which was certain to end fatally in a very few days. The doctor half-hesitatingly revealed to him his hopeless state. "By jingo!" cried he, rousing up at once into the old energy, "I shall *do* the insurance company! I always was a lucky fellow!"

"Even now," reports Mrs Gaskell, a woman well acquainted from her own Northern upbringing, with the asperities of the breed, "a stranger can hardly ask a question without receiving a crusty reply." This was said in 1857. Even now, one might add nearly a century and a half later, the settler from the South, anxious to please in his chosen locality, must not object to being dismissed as one of "the coomers in".

But the soil in which these six hypersensitive children grew was not merely hard favoured. A constant in their lives was the physical and mental cruelty of which the sisters were later to write with such effortless authenticity. The drunken rages of Branwell and the doubtless exasperated severities of their father cannot be used as the sole explanation of how three apparently sheltered young women were able to set down on paper such stuff as later appalled a whole generation of seasoned literary critics. In his decline Branwell was as much a source of sorrowful concern as terror; and it may well be that by the standards of the day Mr Brontë was not an unduly harsh parent.

The answer, of course, is that, though shy and sensitive, the Brontë sisters were not sheltered in the sense that we understand the term. They grew up in an ethos and a society which daily exposed them to violent and savage acts. In their childhood the Luddite riots were things of the recent past – recent enough for Haworth's curate to keep a loaded pistol by his bedside, and to instruct Emily in its use. They may not have witnessed the cockfighting and bull baiting which were still public entertainments in those days. But a more general cruelty to animals which, contrary to the townsman's roseate view of rural life, comes naturally to country folk was clearly a daily spectacle. Emily and Anne write of it with a terrible exactitude of detail that simply cannot be manufactured. And they write about it as they (and Charlotte) write about all such abuses of power in the primitive society that nurtured them: namely that it is to be expected that the strong will, as a matter of course, inflict suffering on the weak.

There may be gothic elements in the Brontë novels; but they have mainly to do with aspects of personal relationships which are not fully explored or understood. When the sisters write of violent behaviour, be it the mental and physical bullying in *Jane Eyre* or the arbitrary destruction of animal life in the work of Emily and Anne, they do so with total authority. By the side of them, the dramatics of a writer like Scott seem mere tushery and bluster.

When Mrs Brontë died on 15th September 1821, her eldest daughter Maria was seven years old. In the agonies of a slow death from what was probably cervical cancer, she had been unable to turn her eyes to a future in heaven, as her husband would have wished her to. In the weeks and days as she slipped away, her constant refrain was for those she was leaving behind : "Oh God my poor children – Oh God my poor children!"

The practical side of running the parsonage now devolved on Aunt Branwell. But Maria, with a maturity far beyond her years, played her part as a mental guide to her siblings. In this she took the lead from her father, who was accustomed to share his preoccupations, political and ecclesiastical, with his children. Since his opinions were always forthright, as well as being argued with the vigour of a truly independent mind, his children lived more completely than most, in the realms of pure thought. His pastoral duties naturally took him often from home and in his absence Maria would read her sisters and brother – and indeed any visitor who might stop by at the parsonage – the accounts of parliamentary debates in the local newspapers.

The effects of this exposure to the events of the day was to generate an extraordinary intellectual precociousness in all the children. Their games were not about the domestic life of their dolls or the fanciful world of gnomes and fairies. Their play was all of Wellington, Bonaparte, Caesar and Hannibal. Their quarrels, if quarrels they had, were heated disputes about the relative merits of these great captains.

Certain myths have grown up about Patrick Brontë's stewardship of this menage for which Mrs Gaskell is largely held to blame by subsequent biographers: that he chopped up one of his wife's dresses which he thought too showy; that he burned some boots of his children's on similar grounds; that he permitted no curtains at the parsonage, thereby rendering it colder and more inhospitable than it might have been; that he let his children eat no meat; that he fired a pistol out of the window every morning to help him to assuage the wrath that daily built up inside him as he contemplated his wifeless state and the circumscription of his ambitions.

These claims can be examined in detail and an opinion more or less safely come to on most of them. In the writing of their personal diary papers his children mention the preparation of meat (and the reservation of a goodly portion of it for the dog on their own whim, so there was obviously plenty of it about). The pistol story has its supporters and detractors. Juliet Barker explains it away by saying that the good curate, keeping as he did a loaded weapon for parsonage and personal defence by his bedside, had perforce to shoot it off each day as the only way of unloading it, given the state of the handgun technology of those times. This is not strictly true. The pistol, which would probably have been a Napoleonic Wars vintage weapon, *could* have been unloaded, albeit with a little difficulty. It could even have been kept loaded for a day or two without danger. In any event an impecunious cleric would hardly have afforded to discharge a pistol ball and a charge of powder per day unless he had some strong impulse to do so.

But none of this matters. It is the kind of detail that bedevils Brontë studies and makes biographies of the sisters swell to inordinate lengths. Even if Mr Brontë was not a perpetually violent parent (and the evidence is that he was not), it takes no great flight of the imagination to accept that he must often (as any single parent of six children would) have had his irascible and arbitrary moments, in which the frustration of disappointed aspirations frothed to the surface and descended on his daughters' heads. But children of a naturally vigorous nature who are brought up in such an atmosphere become inured to it. They have no other standards by which to judge life. And whatever tempests of anger their father may occasionally have given way to, the play of a powerful mind that habitually articulated its thoughts to those around him, must have been, and clearly was, of immense benefit to them.

It is worth mentioning here that Patrick Brontë had had his literary ambitions. *Cottage Poems* were published at his own expense by a Halifax printer in 1811 while he was still curate at Hartshead. Their conventional moralising, expressed in a hidebound verse form, clearly takes its tone from the poetic genre exemplified by Young's *Night Thoughts* and Thomson's *The Seasons*. These, though the nurse-children of a previous century, continued to be popular as 'improving matter' among a general readership, in spite of the revolutionary exertions of the Romantic poets.

A few verses from "Winter-Night Meditations" gives some idea of the characteristic tone of *Cottage Poems*.

> But Summer's gone, and Winter here
> With iron sceptre rules the year –
> Beneath this dark, inclement sky
> How many wanderers faint and die!
> One, flouncing o'er the treacherous snow,
> Sinks in the pit that yawns below!
> Another numbed, with panting lift
> Inhales the suffocating drift!

And creeping cold, with stiffening force,
Extends a third, a pallid corse!

The fate of the volume is not on record. Patrick Brontë did not furnish us with a successor volume although he continued to write occasional verse as well as poems for his own consolation in the quiet hours.

The artificiality of this verse is strangely at odds with the individualistic humanity and the vigorous, and progressive, thought of his sermons. The foregoing and what follows, from his funeral sermon for one of his curates William Weightman, who died of cholera in 1842, are unrecognisable as productions of the same mind.

> In his preaching and practising he was, as every clergyman ought to be, neither distant nor austere, timid nor obtrusive, nor bigoted, exclusive nor dogmatical … He thought it better, and more scriptural, to make the love of God, rather than the fear of hell, the ruling motive for obedience. He did not see why true believers, having the promise of life that now is, as well as that which is to come, should create unto themselves artificial sorrows, and disfigure the garment of gospel peace with the garb of sighing and sadness.

Quite apart from its being a civilised statement of theocentric humanism, this does not sound like the manifesto of one likely to prove a systematically brutal father.

After the death of his wife, Patrick Brontë had made attempts to remarry. The derisive rejection by Mary Burder, already mentioned, was his second – and may have been his third. An earlier application, to Elizabeth Firth, a family friend, had been spurned with almost equal vehemence. Whether or not his addresses on that occasion had been paid with equal lack of tact we cannot know. Gossip next linked him romantically with Isabella Dury, the sister of another local cleric. Whether he actually proposed to her is uncertain. In any event, she made it clear in a letter to a friend that the very idea of marrying a man so encumbered as him, was not to be thought of. Patrick was left to draw the inescapable inference that a forty-seven year old curate with a less than opulent stipend and a large and young family was not going to have the maidens of the parish running after him. After these failures he settled down to single life and to rearing his family with the capable help of his sister in law.

There has been fierce debate over the effects of this combination of guardians on the impressionable minds of such sensitive children. The parameters of this argument are: the notion of a dogmatic Anglican minister perpetually at war with his proselytising Methodist sister-in-law, and fighting ideological and doctrinal battles over the heads and bodies of his children; and the picture of the pair dividing educational and domestic labours between them and subsisting in a species of reasonable harmony that did not greatly disturb their charges. The former scenario sees Anne, in particular, in a state of perpetual terror from her aunt's Calvinistic utterances, a fact which gave rise to the cast of much of her later religious verse.

The truth, as usual lies somewhere between these extremes. The fact is that Aunt Branwell's Cornish Methodism and Patrick's evangelistic Anglicanism would, in practice, not have had a great gulf between them. As we have seen, the line between the Established Church and the Non-Conformists was so blurred in the West Riding that the founding fathers of Methodism had been heard at Haworth church with enthusiasm.

If terrors there were within the walls of Haworth Parsonage they would more likely have stemmed from the atmosphere of unrelenting intellectual rigour created by a father not furnished with much stock of baby talk. Had any one of his children been cursed with that bane of childhood, a sensitive spirit without the immediate means to articulate its perceptions, he might well have been capable of inadvertent cruelty. Obviously, as the famous "mask" episode demonstrates, not one of his children was of a disposition to suffer in this manner.

Briefly (the celebrated episode is set down by Mr Brontë in a letter to Mrs Gaskell of 30th July 1855), their father one day summoned his children and asked each of them to tell him, from behind a mask "in order to make them speak with less timidity" the answer to a series of more or less moral and metaphysical questions. At that time the oldest of them was only ten, but he received from each answers of such ripe wisdom which astonished him. The story of course may have lost little in the telling from a man who in old age still retained a good measure of Irish blarney and naturally wanted to appear in a good light to his daughter's biographer. But there is too much other evidence of his genuine participation in their intellectual development (in particular their military disputes, in which he sometimes had to arbitrate) for it to be dismissed.

The fact is that the Brontë girls were mentally as tough as their father. If any of the family suffered emotional damage from him, it was not "shy" Anne nor "reserved" Emily, but Branwell. And in his case the damage was not from direct mental bullying but rather from the sheer pressure of expectation. The apple of his father's eye, he was given every opportunity to succeed, and converted them all into failure. But Brontë senior cannot be expected to shoulder all the blame for this. As can be detected from the self-regarding tone of his letters and the bombast of his poems there was in Branwell what Isabel Clarke has stigmatised with splendid – though in this instance accurate – Anglo-Saxon prejudice as "the instability and fatal self-esteem of the Celt".

Patrick had this, too, and probably knew it. But in his case the sheer pressure to escape from poverty and an Irish hovel were his salvation.

The mornings of the Brontë children were spent under their father's sporadic instruction, in housework, at their games, and as time went on, at those half-infantile, half-wise Angria and Gondal chronicles which were nevertheless to provide some sort of mysterious basis for their later creativity. In the afternoons, while their father rode about his parish on pastoral business, they were free to roam on the moors, "the elder ones taking thoughtful care for the toddling wee things," as an old woman who had nursed Mrs Brontë in her last illness so charmingly recalled it to Mrs Gaskell in later years. To all of them, this experience was important. To Emily it was something more. In the writings of Charlotte and Anne landscape is a backdrop. To Emily the moors are part of her very being. They and the fierce emotions of their people are germane to everything she wrote. When later separated from them and transplanted to Brussels with Charlotte, she came back with an unbreakable resolve never to leave them again.

The rhythm of the six children's lives at Haworth Parsonage was not permitted to endure long. When they were eight and nine Patrick, recognising the necessity for a formal education for his two oldest daughters, determined to send them to school. This seemed likely to be a prohibitively costly undertaking on a stipend such as his. But in December 1823 a "School for Clergymen's Daughters" had just been advertised in the *Leeds Intelligencer,* offering an education at a price he could afford. This was Cowan Bridge, some distance away in the North West of the county, on the border with Westmorland, and ever afterwards to be notorious as the Lowood of *Jane Eyre.* Its founder, a zealous clergyman, the Rev Carus Wilson, has his own dubious species of immortality as the priggishly cruel Mr Brocklehurst of Charlotte's novel.

Whatever the merits and demerits of the regime at Cowan Bridge, suffice it to say that it killed Maria and Elizabeth and nearly killed Charlotte and Emily, who were sent to join them. Having buried his two oldest children at the ages of ten and eleven respectively, Patrick Brontë came to the conclusion that Cowan Bridge was no place for Charlotte and Emily. After the funerals of Maria and Elizabeth at Haworth in successive months in 1825, the younger daughters did not return to school.

Although Branwell was older than Charlotte it was on her that the mantle of Maria now fell. Maria's death seems, apart from the sheer grief it occasioned, to have thrown her into something of a panic. Charlotte perceived something of moral grandeur in her sister's character which somehow daunted her, and which she was later memorably to translate into that of Helen Burns in *Jane Eyre*. Then, as so often in her life, she had to fight a battle against self-doubt, a struggle exacerbated by weak nerves and poor health.

3 HAWORTH PARSONAGE

AFTER the deaths of Maria and Elizabeth the surviving children were left ever more to their own devices. In between helping with household chores they read voraciously, Wordsworth, Scott and Southey were staple fare. At the age of ten Charlotte was given her mother's copy of Thomas a Kempis's *The Imitation of Christ* – in a translation by John Wesley. From this period date the beginnings of their, at first semi-secret, literary production. There were 'Young Men's Plays' from Branwell and Charlotte, and 'Bed Plays' from Charlotte and Emily. There was a series of magazines from Branwell and Charlotte, and a constant stream of adventures from both, involving their respective heroes, Soult and Wellington.

With the accession to literacy of Anne, these activities took on a collaborative nature, the family splitting into two creative 'camps', Branwell and Charlotte on the one hand, Emily and Anne on the other. The activities of the older pair gradually evolved into the creation of imaginary lands, first the Glasstown Confederacy and then Angria, which were located somewhere in Africa. Emily and Anne replied with Gondal, an island in the North Pacific. These lands were peopled with characters combining fantasy and reality, history, particularly the social history of their area, mythology and a good deal of purely Ruritanian nonsense, described in both prose and poetry. But there was also in these scribblings much that was shrewdly perceptive. In one instance Charlotte makes her aristocratic protagonist give a bantering description of another character which is prophetic of the posturing wastrel Branwell is doomed to become.

These exercises permitted them the exploration of emotions and ideas which Emily, in particular, was later able – with a few deft editings – to present (though much against her will) to the public as fully ripened verse. What is extraordinary about these productions is not so much that they happened, but that the girls continued with this apparently juvenile activity well into maturity. The result is that by the time we come to assessing Emily's poetry it is sometimes impossible to know which elements in it are born of Gondal, and which stem from a maturer sense of reality. Parts of an Emily poem which, in a purely Gondalian context seem to have a merely narrative intention, can, if read without any knowledge of that context, appear to be imbued with a higher spiritual meaning.

But it is difficult to be precise about this. Little of Emily's and Anne's juvenile writing has survived. It would appear that after their deaths Charlotte destroyed much of it – as she is supposed to have destroyed a novel, a successor to *Wuthering Heights*, on which Emily was apparently working. Only the handful of 'diary papers' Emily and Anne wrote together and singly at intervals of several years survive to scatter a few meagre clues as to what was going on in those corners of their minds which were not directly involved with literary activity.

By contrast, all the handwritten productions of Branwell and Charlotte are preserved. They thus give us not only an idea of their creative processes, but also furnish us with an inventory of asides, comments and prejudices on a whole range of topics. The result – combined with the surviving letters of the pair – is that the would-be biographer has Branwell and Charlotte before him as fully-rounded individuals. By contrast Emily and Anne remain shadowy, enigmatic figures, glimpsed only at moments in their lives.

After the disastrous school experiment at Cowan Bridge, the Brontë children spent six years at home. There the girls scrambled into as much of an education as their father had time to impart to them. All the children were also given drawing lessons by John Bradley, one of the founder-members of the newly-established Keighley Mechanics' Institute. Branwell's education was given a more pointed direction by his father. While his sisters' linguistic ambitions at that time extended no further than French, he was sent to tutors and acquired the classics.

From what period, precisely, he showed evidence of the instability that later led to his dependence on alcohol and opium is a moot and always intriguing point. Both his and Charlotte's juvenile writings are replete with references to heavy drinking. But in these it is merely one of the concomitant virtues of the character of a Romantic hero. There is never any suggestion that it is being described from experience. There was to come a time when Charlotte would be far too painfully acquainted with the effects of alcohol abuse ever to want to write as she did in an exuberant jotting of 1829:

> This truly great poet [the figure of Young Soult the Rymer, with whom Branwell closely identified himself]... appears constantly labouring under a state of strong excitement, occasioned by excessive drinking and gambling to which he is unfortunately much addicted ...

By 1831 Charlotte was fifteen. Her father was aware that she would have to make her own living in due course. The only options for someone of her class and education were to become either a governess or schoolteacher. In consequence she was sent back to school again, this time to Roe Head near Mirfield, run by a Miss Margaret Wooler and her sisters. The experience was an altogether happier one than Cowan Bridge. Although at first regarded as a peculiar little creature by her schoolmates, she soon got over her initial homesickness and worked hard at formal subjects such as French and English grammar. She also applied herself diligently to drawing and painting for which, like her sisters, she had considerable natural talent. It was not long before the breadth of her intellectual attainments and knowledge was the wonder of both schoolfellows and teachers. She quickly established herself at the top of her class and carried off a range of prizes and medals.

This success was balm to a shy and retiring spirit which, nevertheless, desired ardently to share its fund of gifts with others. But as important to her self esteem were the friends she made at Roe Head, Mary Taylor and Ellen Nussey. They are important to us, as well, since Charlotte maintained a correspondence with both which tells us much about the petty anxieties and moods which are not part of her 'literary' persona. Ironically it is the correspondence with Ellen which is mostly useful to us in this respect. Mary Taylor was much better equipped to be a soul-mate of Charlotte's. She was a woman of intellect, cultivation and an independent, courageous spirit. Rebelling against the servitude involved in the few employment opportunities for women in Britain, she later emigrated to New Zealand from where she returned after an interval of years, a prosperous woman. Charlotte could and did open her heart to Mary about her deepest feelings. Alas, Mary destroyed almost all the letters Charlotte sent her, so we have only tantalising glimpses of the exchanges between these like minds.

Ellen was a much more commonplace proposition, yet her affectionate nature answered to some need in Charlotte's own more highly-strung one. From her letters to Ellen we learn much about the thousand vexations that made life so often such a trial for a woman of Charlotte's almost morbid sensitivities. When, after Charlotte's marriage to the Rev Arthur Bell Nicholls, her husband required a written pledge of Ellen that she should destroy all Charlotte's letters since they contained unguarded, intimate matter which he considered "dangerous as lucifer matches", Ellen grudgingly consented. Fortunately for us she exercised a woman's prerogative – and readily reneged on her undertaking. The incendiary correspondence continued for the brief remainder of Charlotte's life, without noticeably malign effects.

A year and a half at Roe Head was all Patrick could afford for his daughter. By the summer of 1832 she was back at Haworth where it was now her turn to instruct. Her acquired accomplishments were required by her father to be passed on to her sisters. An early letter to Ellen describes the daily routine:

> An account of one day is an account of all. In the morning, from nine o'clock until half past twelve, I instruct my sisters, and draw; then we walk until dinner-time. After dinner I sew until teatime, and after tea I either write, read or do a little fancy work, or draw, as I please. Thus, in one delightful, though somewhat monotonous course, my life is passed.

Monotonous or not, this was probably as close to contentment as Charlotte was ever to be. With all its proximity to a grim, overstocked graveyard, life within the parsonage walls gave precious moments of calm to a fragile spirit which always seemed to find itself stretched on the rack, as soon as it attempted to achieve anything in the world outside the bounds of Haworth.

It is from this next, relatively tranquil, period in the Brontë sisters' lives that we have the celebrated portrait of them, done by Branwell in 1834 and now hanging in the National Portrait Gallery. It is the nearest we approach to a moment of intimacy with them as a trio. We do not know why Branwell, who had originally featured in the centre of the picture, later painted himself out. One is not inclined to be sorry for it. His other self portraits, even the light-hearted ones, are those of a man with a highly developed sense of his own consequence. That egotistical presence planted firmly in the middle of the portrait must surely have detracted from its quietly haunting quality. As a result of his eliminating himself, the picture falls into two halves: Anne and Emily on the left, Charlotte on the right. They gaze unflinchingly and quite unselfconsciously at us.

It is almost as if we are looking at two different breeds. Charlotte is dumpy, round-faced and homely of feature. It is a pleasant, but not particularly interesting face. The lineaments might be those of a placid young matron. Emily and Anne by contrast transfix us with a riveting intensity of gaze.

If the notion that Anne was somehow a mere passive echo of her sisters in everything she did ever warranted dismissal, it is from this picture. There is a fierce resolve in her eye which, it seems, is no mere accident of execution. In a sketch of her done by Charlotte at roughly the same period, her eye has the same piercing quality. Her tiny mouth which, in any other young woman, might have been a mere rosebud is firmly pursed, as if under the pressure of deep and disturbing thought. A long straight nose, which the Brontë hero, Wellington, himself might have envied, descends from a pair of strongly delineated, frowning eyebrows. It completes an overriding impression of a will not lightly to be deflected from its purposes. Whatever Branwell's other defects, his study is a remarkable perception of the steely qualities of his youngest sister. At the time of the sitting Anne would be no more than fourteen.

The study of Emily is superficially similar. She and Anne share a certain aggressive sharpness of jaw, and the same narrow mouth. From the evidence of this picture she is the only one of the three sisters for whom much claim to beauty could be made. Her nose, not as prominent as either Charlotte's or Anne's, is an undeniably pretty one. We are immediately aware of a large, fair forehead from which her centre-parted hair is pushed back. Her gaze, too, is intense, but the intensity is of a different order from Anne's. There is an almost unearthly light in those eyes, which seem to look not at, but beyond us. This is not that fierce child who could batter her disobedient pet dog with bare hands until it whimpered for mercy, but rather the Emily who loved to wander the moors in solitude, to lounge on her back in the heather and commune lazily with the sky.

In this period, too, we learn more of the Brontë family from an outside source, a visit Ellen Nussey paid to Haworth in 1833. The visit was to Charlotte, but Ellen was clearly captivated by Emily and her indissoluble relationship with Anne. As has been said, Ellen, reminiscing forty years later, is no Boswell but we have to be grateful to her for these glimpses, particularly of Emily. For the fact is that no one of the three sisters is less autobiographical in her fiction. In a Charlotte novel the author's nerve endings, her despairs and her prejudices are never far from the surface. And the nature of Anne's moral being is as clearly delineated in her novels as, say, George Eliot's is in hers. But, largely thanks to Emily's device of using a number of authorial voices, it would be difficult to imagine in detail what *kind* of human being the author of *Wuthering Heights* was in life-over and above the obvious fact that he or she must be extraordinary. Ellen Nussey has left us this description of Emily, setting out for a ramble on the moors.

> She chose a white stuff patterned with thunder and lightning,
> to the scarcely concealed horror of her more sober companions.
> And she looked well in it; a tall, lithe creature with a grace half
> queenly, half untamed in her sudden, supple movements,
> wearing with picturesque negligence her ample purple-splashed
> skirts; her face clear and pale; her very dark and plenteous
> brown hair fastened up behind with a Spanish comb; her large
> grey-hazel eyes, now full of indolent indulgent humour, now
> glimmering with hidden meanings, now quickened into flame
> by a flash of indignation ...

In the general picture of Emily Brontë which is so dominated by the awful details of her death it is refreshing to be able to set off against disease and sickness this portrait of a young woman carelessly revelling in health and strength of body. Spiritual though she was, Emily was totally at home in the physical world. She was the tallest and strongest of the Brontë girls, and much the most active. She loved to stride the hills and scramble on their rocky outcrops. Household chores were meat and drink to her. She would get through mountains of ironing without a murmur. In adulthood she did most of the cooking at the parsonage. She would knead the dough for breadmaking with a German grammar perched behind the bowl. If her father intruded on these domestic chores to ask her to join him in target practice with his pistols, she complied with pleasure. (Like many highly intelligent women she was a good shot.)

Her physical courage was remarkable. Once bitten on the arm by a stray dog to which she had tried to give some water on a day of stifling heat, she repaired without comment to the parsonage kitchen and seared the torn flesh with a red hot iron. All the while not one indication of the excruciating pain she suffered escaped from her compressed lips. To this courage was allied fierce intractability. When told that her bull mastiff, Keeper, was lying upstairs on her bed and could not be dislodged, she marched up to her room and seized the dog by the scruff of the neck. The cowering Charlotte and Anne watched, appalled, as Emily, white to the lips, reappeared at the foot of the stairs with the enraged Keeper contesting every inch of the way with his hind legs while attempting to savage his owner's hand. Determined to punish the beast, but unable to release it while she located a stick, in case it should spring at her throat, Emily pounded its nose and eyes with the fist of her free hand until the former bled and the latter were swollen and closed. Only when Keeper's whimpers signified his submission to her will did she lead him to his accustomed corner where she herself bathed his injuries.

Small wonder that Charlotte, timid and neurotic to the point of hypochondria, was in awe of her. There was a titanic dimension to Emily's character which always eluded her elder sister. Charlotte's assertion to Mrs Gaskell: "I am bound to avow that she had scarcely more practical knowledge of the peasantry among whom she lived than a nun has of the country people that pass her convent gates," may be a well-intentioned attempt to garner for Emily some posthumous forgiveness for having produced such a 'monstrosity' as *Wuthering Heights*. But it is palpably wide of the mark. On every inch of our way over the tremendous emotional crags of Emily's novel we are struck, with almost physical force, by the shock of felt experience.

Of Anne at this period we divine little from Ellen Nussey's comments beyond the fact that she had fair hair, blue eyes and a delicate, almost translucent complexion. What does, however set her apart from both her sisters is a religious sense she seems to have acquired from a quite early age. Though she came to detest the extreme Calvinistic doctrine of the 'elect', sin was a reality to her, as was the cause of sin. Thus the moral universe of her novels is a place of far greater certitude than that of either of her sisters: Charlotte perpetually unsure but adhering more or less to a 'conventional' Anglican position; Emily breaking all bounds and communing with the Almighty on her own terms. This does not automatically make either Anne or her novels less interesting. She felt too deeply, experienced life too painfully, for that.

But whatever the differences in their personalities, the Brontë sisters were from the earliest moments of their articulacy, a trio of writers in the making. At eight o'clock every evening Mr Brontë, having read the prayers, locked and barred the doors and bade his children not to stay up too late. He then mounted the stairs, pausing to wind the clock on the landing and retired to rest.

Another hour, which the girls devoted to sewing, now elapsed, while they waited for the announcement that Aunt Branwell, too, was for bed. Then began the famous ritual that, until death parted them, was to become the most important part of their day together. Extinguishing the parlour candles for economy's sake, the three sisters would pace backwards and forwards in the firelight, discussing their hopes and apprehensions, plans for obtaining employment and, as time went on, plots for new novels.

This period of relative tranquillity could not be allowed to continue indefinitely. Charlotte had to earn a living and in the summer of 1835 she returned to Roe Head where Miss Wooler had offered her a teaching post. Emily went with her as a pupil. But she found this first experience of being away from her home, from her beloved moors and the wellsprings of her creative being such a devastating one that, in a remarkable testament to the power of mind over body, she began, literally, to waste away. The rapid decline of her vigorous constitution and the daily reproach of her pallid face and emaciated figure convinced Charlotte that school would kill Emily as surely as it had killed her sisters. Her father had no intention of losing another daughter to the good cause of education, and in little more than two months she was allowed to return to Haworth. She was replaced at Roe Head by Anne who, homesick though she may have been, had a nature more amenable to the routine and discipline of a school.

The story of Charlotte's life over the next dozen years is a constant battle to find a raison d'être, against her native pessimism, self-doubt and a rooted lack of self esteem. In many ways she comes over as the least attractive of the three sisters. (She has exposed herself to so much greater a degree in her letters that the comparison may not be a fair one. By contrast, Emily's few and curt extant epistles give away nothing.) But the spectacle of her overcoming her mental frailties and the weaknesses of a body racked with disorders, many of which were clearly psychogenic in origin, to propel her and her sisters into the pages of literary history is a deeply moving one.

With her shy, shrinking nature she was constitutionally unfit to be a teacher. It was a job which, both at Roe Head and later in Brussels, subjected her to daily agonies of mind. She was unfit, indeed, to be almost anything practical – however mundane. A pile of ironing, a dirty floor clamouring for a good scrub, a large bowl of potatoes to be peeled for that night's supper, all grist to Emily's mill, were anathema to her. And she had not that tremendous power of mind which enabled Emily – and to a lesser extent Anne – to sustain long periods of solitude. She could be captious and fretful. She quarrelled with Miss Wooler who admired and loved her; she was frequently out of charity with Haworth, as her letters show; later, when she had gained fame and the respect of her peers, she found London literary life an ordeal which made her physically ill. But she remained true to herself. And it is to her unswerving sense of purpose that the world owes its knowledge of the literary phenomenon of the Brontës.

During her period at Roe Head she took the first steps to convert the secret creativity of the Haworth quiet hours into a literary career. Shortly after Christmas 1836 she sent off a number of her poems to Robert Southey at his home in the Lake District and invited his opinion of them. The Poet Laureate's reply was a mixture of critical acuity and kind condescension. He recognised the merits of her verse. It is a pity he did not live to see the publication of *Jane Eyre* and ponder again his famous injunction to its author.

> Literature cannot be the business of a woman's life: & it ought not to be. The more she is engaged in her proper duties, the less leisure she will have for it, even as an accomplishment & a recreation. To those duties you have not yet been called, & when you are you will be less eager for celebrity.

Charlotte did not long enough survive her later acquaintanceship with "her proper duties" for us to know whether she would have succeeded in extending her literary reputation. In any event, she already had her celebrity by that time. But we must be thankful that she did not adhere to the terms of the resolution contained in her reply to Southey.

> I trust I shall never more feel ambitious to see my name in print – if the wish should rise I'll look at Southey's autograph and suppress it.

Meanwhile Branwell had been trying to give a similar impetus to his literary career. He had for some time been pestering the editor of *Blackwood's Magazine* first to publish his work and then, with extraordinary effrontery, to, as it were, fire one of his major contributors, the Scottish pastoral poet James Hogg, and employ him, Patrick Branwell Brontë, instead. These letters, which were received in dignified silence, became more and more importunate in their tone.

> Will you Still so wearisomely refuse me a word, when you can neither know what you refuse or whom you are refusing? Do you think your Magazine so perfect that no addition to its power would be either possible or desirable? – Is it pride that accentuates you – or custom – or prejudice? – Be a Man – Sir! and think no more of these things!

The editor of *Blackwood's* kept his distance from this tirade, too.

Shortly after Charlotte had written to Southey, Branwell addressed himself and a specimen of his verse to the Lakeland's other literary lion, William Wordsworth. Wordsworth cannot have taken long to discern the inherent instability in a nature which could at once grossly flatter him and at the same time imprudently assert

> Surely in this day when there is not a writing poet worth a sixpence the feild [sic] must be open if a better man can step forward.

This, too, went unanswered. True, the year was 1837 and Wordsworth had been to all intents and purposes creatively dead long since. But he would not have thanked a Branwell Brontë for reminding him of that.

Balked for the moment in his literary ambitions, Branwell frittered the rest of the year flirting with Freemasonry. Then, about the middle of 1838 he reverted to a career he had previously intended to follow, that of painter. In addition to the art lessons he had taken with his sisters, he had had instruction with a local Royal Academy trained man, William Robinson from Leeds. In 1835 he had applied unsuccessfully to study at the Royal Academy. It was a somewhat fanciful gesture, since his fitful application to his art meant that he was woefully short of assembling the required portfolio.

Nevertheless, using his local contacts and supported by his father, in the spring of 1838 he set up as a portrait painter in Bradford. An essentially clubbable, garrulous character, he had no difficulty making friends who could help him and put commissions his way. Among these was the celebrated Halifax sculptor J. B. Leyland, who remained a lifelong friend. But it seems that the lure of Bradford's social life was too much for him. Within twelve months he was back in Haworth with a taste for bar-room philosophising of that sort which requires copious alcoholic lubrication of the larynx. It is from this point in his life that we derive the firm impression of drinking habits which have gone beyond control. Almost every opportunity he is given from here onwards ends in that kind of failure which is patently self-induced.

In June 1840 he is dismissed, after only six months, from a decent post as tutor to the sons of a Lancashire county magistrate. He is nevertheless fortunate enough to obtain posts on the railway, first as assistant clerk at Sowerby Bridge station and then as clerk in charge at Luddenden Foot. From the latter he is dismissed in March 1842 when discrepancies are found in his accounts. In the next year he obtains a post as tutor to the Robinsons of Thorp Green, near York, where Anne is governess. From this he is dismissed after eighteen months when his employer discovers an intrigue between Branwell and his wife.

This dismal employment record from a man so much better qualified to get work than his sisters, in the climate then prevailing, suggests a life on the skids. It is difficult to credit Juliet Barker's contention that Branwell's alcoholism dates only from his despair at not being able to marry Mrs Robinson. He learns of the impossibility of this only after her husband's death in May 1846. By September 1848 he is dead.

Death through alcoholism is not normally accomplished in such a short time. With his now nonexistent and his father's slender means, Branwell certainly could not have afforded it.

Charlotte habitually found work a struggle, too, but for different reasons. Life itself grated on her and her almost pathological shyness was only exacerbated by the necessity to teach and the continual negotiation with human beings on all levels that involved. She well described what this struggle for mere existence cost her in one of her letters to Ellen Nussey.

> Some of my greatest difficulties lie in things that would appear to you comparatively trivial. I find it so hard to repel the rude familiarity of children. I find it so difficult to ask either servants or mistress for anything I want, however much I want it. It is less pain for me to endure the greatest inconvenience than to go into the kitchen to request its removal. I am a fool. Heaven knows I cannot help it!

In the end this self-avowed hypochondria got completely the better of her and in the spring of 1838 she left Roe Head and returned home. There were to be further attempts at holding down governesses' positions over the next few years. But most of the time between then and the great expedition to Brussels in 1842 was spent at Haworth parsonage.

Shy, she may have been, but, as we have seen, she and her sisters hardly led cloistered lives. As *Shirley* so vividly conveys, the society in which they lived may have been rude and sometimes rough, but it undeniably *was* a society. And its doings impinged on them constantly. One of its most intrusive components was the opposite sex and their attentions, and none of the girls was immune to that. Nor is there any evidence that they wanted to be. Charlotte had a number of proposals of marriage in her life before the one she finally accepted. Her letters to Ellen are often flirtatious on the subject of sexual attraction. From the material available – a not, one imagines, very personable bunch of local curates – she is able, in a letter of May 1840, to give her friend sage advice on love and marriage.

> Do not be persuaded to marry a man you can never respect – I do not say love, because, I think, if you can respect a person before marriage, moderate love at least will come after; and as to intense passion, I am convinced that it is no desirable feeling. In the first place, it seldom or never meets with a requital; and, in the second place, if it did, the feeling would be only temporary.

The wisdom of twenty-four. Yet in her own life it was the passion, intellectual and moral as well as emotional, which she was later to feel for a man like Heger, that was her true currency in these matters. And it is this that flashes out from the pages of her novels.

Charlotte had already, in March of the previous year, turned down Ellen's brother, the Rev Henry Nussey, when she wrote her advice to her friend. In spite of the "decided negative" with which she did so, they were to remain correspondents and friends. Before the year was out she had had a second proposal, this time from a young Irish curate called Pryce. This proposal, by letter and based upon the acquaintanceship of a single afternoon, had, it is true, a somewhat whimsical quality about it. "I've heard of love at first sight but this beats all," commented Charlotte to Ellen. Pryce, too, was rejected.

Romance was also in the air for the other sisters, Its source was a curate called William Weightman who, in May 1839, was appointed by the increasingly infirm Mr Brontë to help him in his pastoral duties. We have already heard Patrick Brontë's testimonial to Weightman's sterling qualities as a clergyman. He was also a handsome devil and a ladies' man. A pencil sketch of him by Charlotte shows a high forehead, firm nose, handsome mouth, resolute chin and a mien altogether conscious of its merits and power to please.

A certain amount of mythology has grown up around the character of Weightman. The assumption that Anne was deeply in love with him and never really got over his death, leads the speculative field by some distance. But the honour of loving him most has been ascribed by different commentators to all the sisters at some point. In Anne's and Emily's case, deeply-felt verses have been exhumed to 'prove' the case. Undoubtedly such a man must have caused a flutter from time to time in their susceptible hearts – as he did in those of Ellen Nussey and several other young ladies of the district. But all the evidence is that he was merely an agreeable flirt, who spread his favours so wide without any attempt to disguise his doing so, that he is not likely seriously to have disturbed the composure of such deep-souled women. Charlotte's light-hearted verse reply to the Valentine cards he sent them all surely says it all:

> A Rowland for your Oliver
>   We think you've justly earned;
> You sent us each a valentine,
>   Your gift is now returned.

> We cannot write or talk like you;
>   We're plain folks every one;
> You've played a clever trick on us,
>   We thank you for the fun.

It is impossible to imagine that the heartfelt notes of Anne's "Life seems more sweet that thou did'st live…" or Emily's "Cold in the earth and the deep snow piled above thee…" could possibly have their origins in such a man – though of course they may well have used the idea of the shocking waste of his too early death as their starting point. But such is the jackdaw-like nature of creativity.

4 BRUSSELS AND AFTER

THE three sisters had been toying for some time with the idea of setting up a school. In 1841 impetus was given to their fledgling plans when Aunt Branwell offered to support them financially if they could show her that their arrangements were soundly based. At about the same time Miss Wooler asked Charlotte if she would like to run her school, now at Dewsbury Moor.

But by this time Charlotte was already running with another idea. After several more abortive attempts at proving herself as a governess, she was restless for change. A letter from Mary Taylor, on holiday on the Continent with her brother, crystallised in Charlotte the idea of going abroad too, to study foreign languages. There was an element of sheer selfishness and a desire for novelty in all this. But she rationalised it, not totally disingenuously, by telling Aunt Branwell that the acquisition of the ability to teach French would, really, be a *sine qua non* of any school they might set up themselves, and that the money spent on sending her and Emily to Brussels to do that would be a sound investment.

The idea carried the day. So often in the grip of virtual paralysis when it came to small things, Charlotte seemed to find an access of energy which swept aside such considerations as the wisdom of transplanting Emily to Brussels when the experience of mere Roe Head had almost proved fatal. (Anne, at this time installed as a governess with the Robinsons, was not a candidate for the trip. Emily's opinion of the venture has not been recorded.)

On 15th February 1842, escorted by their father, the pair arrived at the Pensionnat Heger, in Brussels. It was the beginning of an experience which was to furnish Charlotte with the setting for two of her novels and give us one of her most striking protagonists. Yet although the conception and execution of the plan were Charlotte's, one of its most interesting results for us is that it provides us with more valuable glimpses of Emily, from an independent and impartial source.

Constantin Heger, who ran the pensionnat with his wife, was a man of intellect, passion and perception. After surveying his two peculiarly-dressed English charges he came to the conclusion that they were individuals of no common mental capacity. He suggested that their French studies should proceed not along the conventional path of grammar, vocabulary and translation exercises, but by hearing him read passages from the French masters of style and attempting to emulate them. Emily immediately set her teeth against the proposal, saying it would destroy her native prose style. Heger had his way, but at the same time received a first intimation of the stubbornness of his formidable pupil. He came to rate her intellectual and imaginative faculties above those of Charlotte. He was later to say to Mrs Gaskell that Emily had a head for logic and a capability of argument unusual in a man, and rare indeed in a woman. Indeed:

> She should have been a man – a great navigator. Her powerful reason would have deduced new spheres of discovery from the knowledge of the old; and her strong imperious will would never have been daunted by opposition or difficulty; never have given way but with life.

But he also recognised a "stubborn tenacity of will which rendered her obtuse to all reasoning where her own wishes or her own sense of right were concerned". This tenacity enabled her, at least, so to absorb herself in her studies that in Brussels she suffered none of the dramatic psychogenic illness which had brought her so low at Roe Head.

Charlotte was much more biddable. She liked being a pupil again, after the strains of teaching. While she felt the force of Emily's arguments against Heger's proposals she felt they ought to submit, as he was their 'master'. (How often that term later recurs in her novels, when her women consider their men.) For his part, Heger admired Emily's gifts. But he liked Charlotte more. She obliged him with floods of tears when he castigated her efforts as being *peu correcte*, and this appealed to the domineering male in him.

In fact, his methods were a boon to her. Contact with French authors eliminated from her prose style the florid tendencies of her Angria jottings. By compelling her to write about specific historical episodes in French, and subjecting every sentence she wrote to stringent analysis, Heger helped her towards the faculty of graphic reportage which characterises her novels at their best. This submission to his principles of composition was to become psychological dependence and, finally, uncontrollable love for Heger. But for the moment it benefited her immeasurably.

The sisters kept apart from the Belgian girls at the Pensionnat Heger. Those well-heeled daughters of the bourgeoisie mocked their outlandish appearance – Charlotte, drab and dumpy, Emily, tall and seemingly ungainly in the high-waisted, figure-clinging dresses and gigantic gigot sleeves of a former sartorial age. Emily preserved an icy indifference: "I wish to be as God made me."

Charlotte developed an almost pathological dislike of Roman Catholicism and the character of her charges. We instinctively recoil from a judgement which stigmatises virtually all the school's inmates as having "a character singularly cold, selfish, animal and inferior". Unfortunately this antipathy spills over, unchecked, into *Villette,* where, much to the detriment of the novel, it operates merely at the level of Anglo-Saxon/Protestant propaganda.

Charlotte also took it upon herself to record the "strong recoil of her [Emily's] upright, heretic and English spirit from the gentle Jesuistry of the foreign and Romish system". Yet, while she could not be bothered to engage with them mentally, there is no evidence that Emily ever uttered any objection against her schoolfellows on the grounds of their race, religion or sartorial habits. Interestingly, in view of her constant criticisms of Belgian worldly vanity, it was Charlotte who decided to spruce up her image, adopting a more up-to-date Continental style of dress which did, in truth, better suit her short but not unshapely figure.

At the Pensionnat Heger, Charlotte and Emily made rapid progress in French and German. They also had lessons in drawing and on the piano. Heger rated Emily's gifts on the keyboard so highly that he thought there was nothing she might not achieve in that sphere. The girls had intended to stay in Brussels only six months. When, in August 1842, they were offered the opportunity to stay for another six months *au pair,* Charlotte teaching English and Emily giving some piano lessons in exchange for free study themselves, Charlotte accepted with alacrity.

But they were not to see out the second six months. On October 29th Aunt Branwell died of what biographers are content to describe as "an internal obstruction", presumably some form of bowel cancer. Charlotte and Emily had already learned that she was gravely ill and had made plans to return to Haworth. They arrived too late to be at her funeral.

They brought back to their father a testimonial letter from Heger in which he stressed their accomplishments and begged Mr Brontë to allow them to return to Brussels when a decent interval had elapsed. Charlotte had already resolved within herself so to do. Emily was equally deeply resolved never to be parted from Haworth and its moors again. Without Aunt Branwell to run the parsonage she was quite happy to take on herself the whole domestic burden. If she needed further instruction in languages, she administered it to herself in between or during the performance of the daily household chores. Most important, she was back in touch with the sources of her creativity.

From Aunt Branwell's will, the three sisters received £300 each. Notwithstanding Charlotte's determination to return to Brussels for a further period, plans to start a school were dormant, not defunct. Emily, who had a good head for such matters, took over the management of this legacy (which was invested in the York and Midland Railway) with a view to preserving it for the day it would be needed to finance the project. Early in the New Year, 1843, Anne returned to Thorp Green, accompanied by Branwell who was to take up his new post there as tutor to the Robinsons' children. Shortly afterwards, Charlotte left for Brussels.

These were to be the last attempts of any of the parties to earn a living from conventional employment. After less than a year at the Pensionnat Heger, Charlotte returned home in utter misery. Eighteen months after that, Anne was back at Haworth for good, sickened by the raffish tenor of life at Thorp Green. Within another month Branwell had followed her, though, as we have seen, his departure was involuntary. By that time, balked at all points, the three sisters were forced back on what they did best – their writing.

Charlotte had returned to Brussels in high hopes. She was buoyed by the exhilarating awareness of possessing mental capacities that were appreciated by Heger in a way they could never have been by a Yorkshire curate. At the pensionnat she was given greater status as a teacher than before. She was even permitted to teach English to her 'master' and his brother-in-law. But as the frequency and tone of her correspondence: to Ellen, to Emily, to Branwell, indicates, she felt isolated almost from the outset. Her intellectual dependency on Heger swiftly developed into an emotional one and from that into uncontrolled love. This only increased her sense of isolation; Heger's wife, a canny woman who through spying on her pupils had made herself mistress of their inmost thoughts, made certain, too, that this intense little Englishwoman was to be allowed no *tête à tête* with her idol. By May 1843 Charlotte was dolefully reporting to Emily:

> Of late days, Mr and Mde Heger rarely speak to me, and I really don't pretend to care a fig for any body else in the establishment. You are not to suppose by that expression that I am under the influence of warm affection for Mde Heger. I am convinced she does not like me – why I can't tell, not do I think she herself has any definite reason for the aversion ...

In the light of the passionate avowal of love for Heger contained in the letters she later wrote from Haworth, this last seems disingenuous. But it may not be. Heger had awakened an ardent admiration in her for his intellectual gifts. Well able to fend off the lesser claims of such tolerably accomplished men as Weightman, she had no defence against an attachment of a power she had never known before. At this stage she probably hardly knew she was falling in love. The tone of her closing remarks to Emily on this occasion suggests religious rather than emotional idolatry:

> I fancy he has taken to considering me as a person to be let alone – left to the error of her ways; and consequently he has in a great measure withdrawn the light of his countenance...

But Madame Heger was taking no chances on Charlotte's admiration of her husband having a purely religious character. She saw to it that the light of his countenance remained steadfastly withdrawn.

Charlotte now endured a summer of such spiritual wretchedness that one evening, while in the Cathedral of Ste Gudule she approached the confessional and, while admitting that she was a Protestant, spilled out her sense of desolation to the priest within. When she had finished he asked her to come to his house the following day. In the upshot, her Protestant reflexes prevented her from taking this instant of flirtation with Catholicism any further. But by the autumn she could stand her mental prostration no longer, and in October offered her resignation to Madame Heger. Madame accepted it, but was vehemently overruled by her husband. Whatever his motives – and it seems that they were honourable; he thought it a pity she should leave before formally completing her studies – it would have been better if he had not thrown her what she was bound to take as an emotional lifeline. After two more desultory months she again tendered her resignation. Heger did the decent thing and furnished her with a sort of teaching diploma, to which was attached the seal of the Athénée Royal. Over the next year he was the recipient of several impassioned letters from her at Haworth. Their tone is the desperate one of unrequited love. Coming from a woman of such high mental attainments, their total self abasement makes painful reading.

> I know that you will be impatient when you read this letter ...
> I do not seek to justify myself, I submit to every kind of reproach
> – all that I know is that I will not resign myself to losing the
> friendship of my master ... Monsieur, the poor do not need

much to live – they only ask for the crumbs of bread which fall from the rich man's table – but if one refuses them these crumbs of bread they die of hunger – Nor do I need much affection from those I love but you once showed me a little interest when I was your pupil in Brussels – and I cling onto preserving that little interest – I cling on to it as I cling on to life …

The frantic, incoherent sentences, the unashamed nakedness of feeling are doubtless those of all hopeless loves down the ages. But it is unimaginative to dismiss them as merely infatuated, as they have been. The agony of mind to which they give witness asks for a moment of silent thought from anyone who has ever been compelled, as this high-principled woman now was, to a confession of such total loss of self-respect. They are a testament to the power of that – almost inexplicable – dark side of love which makes its victims willingly drink deep of humiliation.

Back in Haworth Charlotte tried to repair the breaches in her tormented mental fabric by re-igniting the project for a school. With her father's health and sight declining, it was impossible to think of leaving him unattended. Therefore, such a school would have to be at the parsonage. With some alterations to its rooms there was just space to accommodate an economically viable number of pupils, and the sisters would not be at the expense of paying rent.

There is something touching about the completeness of their failure in the school idea. Prospectuses for "The Misses Brontë's Establishment" (in splendid Gothic script) were sent out, with its plan for THE BOARD AND EDUCATION OF A LIMITED NUMBER OF YOUNG LADIES, followed by a schedule, costed no doubt by Emily, of lessons to be offered and fees to be charged. It concluded "A Quarter's Notice, or a Quarter's Board, is required previous to the Removal of a Pupil".

They need not have bothered. No one came. The feared wranglings over a quarter's board in lieu of notice never took place. For the last three months of 1844 Charlotte and Emily (Anne was with Branwell at Thorp Green) waited at the parsonage for their school project to

43

show some signs of becoming a reality, and then quietly gave it up. Charlotte put the best face on it that she could: "it teaches us experience and an additional knowledge of the world". Emily was deeply involved in her poetry.

Contemporaneously with the passage of Charlotte's great love, Branwell was having the great affair of *his* life at Thorp Green. Mrs Gaskell has set the tone for our view of this by laying the blame squarely on Mrs Robinson (thereby incurring the threat of libel from her). The topic has been a battleground for literary biographers ever since. It need not be.

Like so many men, Branwell was of that shallow and self-regarding type of seducer which projects its own ego onto the supposedly beloved object, and then wallows in the delicious results obtained. There is no doubt that he had Mrs Robinson's complete cooperation in this. He was a younger man, attractive, eccentric, capable of entertaining her conversationally and sexually in a way that her terminally ill husband could not. It is equally clear that she had no intention of taking the affair seriously, much less of marrying him after her husband's death. A moment's thought would have told him this. But the language of his letters is that of total (and willing?) self-delusion.

This (from a letter to his sculptor friend J. B. Leyland) after hearing of Mr Robinson's death and (as he supposes) his will's interdicting their marriage.

> Well, my dear Sir, I have got my finishing stroke at last – and I feel stunned into marble by the blow.
>
> I have this morning received a long, kind and faithful letter from the medical gentleman who attended Mr R. in his last illness and who has since had an interview with one I can never forget.
>
> He knows me <u>well </u>and he pities my case most sincerely …
> When he mentioned my name she stared at him and fainted. When she recovered she in turns dwelt on her inextinguishable love for me – her horror at having been the first to delude me into wretchedness, and her agony at having been the cause of

the death of her husband... Her sensitive mind was totally wrecked. She wandered into talking of entering a nunnery; and the Doctor fairly debars me from all hope ...

I am not a whiner, dear Sir, but when a young man like myself has fixed his soul on a being worthy of all love – and who for years has given him all love, pardon him for boring a friend with a misery that has only one black end.

I fully expected a change of the will – and difficulties placed in my way by rich and powerful men, but I hardly expected the hopeless ruin of the mind that I loved even more than its body.

This is a man to whom reality has been a stranger long since. A clandestine intrigue has become the love of years. The will, altered to sunder tragic lovers, is the stuff of melodrama. The overwrought sentiment is that of the Victorian minor novel, seen at its sickliest in Caroline Archer Clive's *Why Paul Ferroll killed his Wife*. The difference, as anyone can see, between this and Charlotte's outburst to Heger is that whereas she is confronting the dreadful truth of her situation, Branwell's version of what is happening to him is pure fantasy.

Mrs Robinson must be given top marks for creativity, assuming she dictated the touching scenario her ex-lover was so eager to swallow hook, line and sinker. But she had no intention of marrying a ne'er-do-well like Branwell, simply because he had satisfied her bodily needs in an hour of sexual frustration.

Her nunnery plans were, somehow, never activated. Lady Scott, the wife of Sir Edward Scott of Great Barr Hall, near Birmingham, was known to be failing. A title and wealth were now her aims. When the first Lady Scott died, Mrs Robinson stepped into her shoes with alacrity. She married Sir Edward Scott on 8th November 1848, six weeks after Branwell's death. Her comment, if any, on that occurrence is unrecorded. It seems hardly likely she jeopardised her situation by even noticing it.

5 THE ROAD TO AUTHORSHIP

IN THE seeming wreck of the Brontës' hopes for advancing themselves any further, we are as well off with Charlotte's version of what suddenly redeemed them from obscurity, as any other. It is contained in a *Biographical Notice of Ellis and Acton Bell,* with which she prefaced the 1850 reprint of *Wuthering Heights* and *Agnes Grey.*

> One day, in the autumn of 1845, I accidently lighted on an MS. volume of verse in my sister Emily's handwriting. Of course, I was not surprised, knowing she could and did write verse: I looked it over and something more than surprise seized me – a deep conviction that these were not common effusions, nor at all like the poetry women generally write. I thought them condensed and terse, vigorous and genuine. To my ear they also had a peculiar music – wild, melancholy, and elevating.
>
> My sister Emily was not a person of demonstrative character, nor one on the recesses of whose mind and feelings, even those nearest and dearest to her could, with impunity, intrude unlicensed; it took hours to reconcile her to the discovery I had made, and days to persuade her that such poems merited publication I knew however, that a mind like hers could not be without some latent spark of honourable ambition, and refused to be discouraged in my attempts to fan that spark to flame. Meantime, my younger sister quietly produced some of her own compositions, intimating that since Emily's had given me pleasure, I might like to look at hers. I could not but be a partial judge, yet I thought that these verses, too, had a sweet, sincere pathos of their own.

The rest, in contemporary parlance, is history. Still, even at this distance we cannot help but quail afresh for Charlotte, for the roasting Emily evidently gave her for her intrusion. The tempest of wrath continued for some hours; obdurate resistance to Charlotte's plans, for much longer. But we must be grateful that the meddler persisted, whatever the cost to Emily's feelings. To Charlotte we owe the Brontës as we have them today. Without her initiative, from whatever selfish motives of frustrated ambition it proceeded, the novels might never have seen the light of day in the short span of life that remained to each of the sisters. She was never under any illusions about the value of her contribution to a volume of verse which, they agreed, should be offered for publication as being the work of three brothers, with whom Charlotte, as their negotiating agent, was acquainted.

The enterprise was what today would be regarded as a species of vanity publishing, inasmuch as they paid for it themselves. But this was not unusual for 'slim volumes' of verse at that time, the agreement being that they would recoup royalties once the publication price, £31 10s (plus another £5 Charlotte had later to shell out for unforeseen expenses), had been reached by sales. And, unlike the productions of modern vanity publishing, the volume would be considered a serious one and the publisher, in this case Aylon and Jones of Paternoster Row, London, would send copies out for review. *Poems by Currer Ellis and Acton Bell* was published in 1846 and received good and on the whole perceptive notices in a number of the journals of the day. No reviewer detected, as many reviewers of the novels later did, that the authors were women. Some singled out Emily's contribution as being the most striking and individual. A notice in the *Critic* of 4th July 1846 was the fulfilment of Charlotte's heart's desire:

> … it is long since we have enjoyed a volume of such genuine poetry as this. Amid the heaps of trash and trumpery in the shape of verses, which lumber the table of the literary journalist, this small book of some 170 pages has come like a ray of sunshine, gladdening the eye with present glory and the heart with promise of bright hours in store. Here we have good, wholesome, refreshing, vigorous poetry – no sickly affectations, no tedious imitations of familiar strains, but original thoughts expressed in the true language of poetry …

The *Athenaeum* of the same date was less fulsome but more discriminating:

> The second book on our list furnishes another example of a
> family in which appears to run the instinct of song. It is shared,
> however, by the three brothers – as we suppose them to be – in
> very unequal proportions; requiring in the case of Acton Bell,
> the indulgences of affection... and rising, in that of Ellis, into
> an inspiration, which may yet find audience in the outer world.

As we shall see, this was less than fair to Anne, who has a slight, but genuine, poetic gift.

A modest critical success, the *Poems* were a commercial disaster. Precisely two copies of the book were sold in the first year. The sisters never recouped their outlay and in the following year Charlotte sent a number of complimentary copies of the volume to De Quincy and Hartley Coleridge, among others, by way of casting bread upon the waters.

The failure did not matter. Seeing their work in print had shown even the obdurately reclusive Emily proof that a creativity like hers could not remain a private matter.

All three sisters had been working at novels during the spring and on the very day of the *Athenaeum* notice Charlotte, as Currer Bell, wrote to a London publisher Henry Colburn offering "a work of fiction in 3 vols... three tales each occupying a volume". The three were *The Professor, Wuthering Heights* and *Agnes Grey*. They were never to see the light of day in that form. Emily's novel was far too long for it to have made one element, with the others, of the three-volume package of the day. But by this time she had totally overcome her scruples about pushing her work. The entrepreneur in her was at last roused. *Wuthering Heights* and *Agnes Grey* in tandem were of precisely the right length to come into three volumes. When it became clear that an "ignominious and abrupt dismissal" was to be the fate of the three stories whenever they were touted in harness, she and Anne closed with an offer from T. C. Newby to publish their two novels together. They were not wise in their choice of publisher. They had to pay for publication and were later to suffer from some sharp practice from Newby when he tried to pretend that the three Bells were one person and cash in on the success of *Jane Eyre*. But it was a launch as novelists.

In the meantime, *The Professor* was "plodding its weary round in London" receiving a decided negative at each port of call. Eventually and providentially, it arrived at the offices of Smith, Elder, a house containing men of discrimination and honour, as well as business acumen. They declined to publish *The Professor,* but instead of replying to its author in "two hard, hopeless lines, intimating that Messrs Smith and Elder 'were not disposed to publish the MS'," as Charlotte was later to recall, they fairly discussed its merits and intimated that a three-volume novel from C. Bell "would meet with careful attention".

With a rapidity the more astonishing for the fact that she had to write in gloomy lodgings in Manchester, where she had accompanied her father to have a cataract operation, Charlotte now finished *Jane Eyre*, on which she had been working, and posted it off to Smith, Elder.

George Smith, the firm's energetic young proprietor, has memorably described the impact of the contents of this unimposing paper parcel.

> After breakfast on Sunday morning I took the MS of 'Jane Eyre' to my little study and began to read it. The story quickly took me captive. Before twelve o'clock my horse came to the door, but I could not put the book down. I scribbled two or three lines to my friend [with whom he had promised to go out riding], saying I was very sorry that circumstances had arisen to prevent my meeting him, sent the note off by my groom and went on reading the MS. Presently the servant came to tell me that luncheon was ready; I asked him to bring me a sandwich and a glass of wine and went on reading 'Jane Eyre'. Dinner came; for me the meal was a hasty one, and before I went to bed that night I had finished reading the manuscript. The next day we wrote to 'Currer Bell' accepting the book for publication.

Thus was ushered in that *annus mirabilis* in the history of the English novel, 1847. *Jane Eyre* was published in October, actually beating into print *Wuthering Heights* and *Agnes Grey* which, thanks to the dilatoriness of Newby, had to wait until the following month.

Jane Eyre was warmly reviewed by most critics, and found a favour with the public it has never lost. Thackeray, one of Charlotte's heroes, declared that he could not put it down, and received the compliment of having its second printing dedicated to him. (It was a compliment he could actually have done without; his own marital circumstances bore an unhealthily close relationship to those of Rochester, though Charlotte was not to know that.) George Eliot and G. H. Lewes were also fascinated – though for very different reasons. For Lewes it was "a book after our own heart". Eliot had reservations about the degree of self-sacrifice involved in the situations of both Jane and Rochester, and wished the characters "would talk a little less like the heroes and heroines of police reports".

In a surprisingly short time the reputation of Charlotte's novel had made its way back to the Haworth locality where her use of Cowan Bridge School as the Lowood of *Jane Eyre* was immediately rumbled by a local parson. In America, likewise, it was a critical and commercial success.

Both *Wuthering Heights* and *Agnes Grey* puzzled reviewers. Many were appalled by Emily's novel. For E. G. Whipple in *North American Review,* its author appeared "to take a morose satisfaction in developing a full and complete science of human brutality". Even reading it seven years later, Dante Gabriel Rossetti described it as being " ...a fiend of a book – an incredible monster... The action is laid in hell ..." *Douglas Jerrold's Weekly Newspaper* came as close as any, at that time, to perceiving its unique strengths – and difficulties. "*Wuthering Heights* is a strange sort of book, – baffling all regular criticism; yet, it is impossible to begin and not finish it; and quite as impossible to lay it aside afterwards, and say nothing about it."

Agnes Grey was less roughly handled, though since it was read after *Wuthering Heights* one senses it benefited from a certain emotional exhaustion in the reviewers. Its virtues tended to be described as a series of negatives. Its language was "less ambitious and less repulsive" than that of *Wuthering Heights* (*New Monthly Magazine*). It was "a somewhat coarse imitation of one of Miss Austin's [sic] charming stories" (*Atlas*). While *Douglas Jerrold's Weekly* commended only its protagonist's description of "the minute torments and incessant tediums of her life".

But whatever these vicissitudes of critical fortune, the name and *oeuvre* of Bell/Brontë was ineradicably on the literary map. Changes of taste in succeeding ages were never to remove it.

What, in the face of this extraordinary burst of creative and promotional activity from his sisters, was Branwell doing? The question has to be asked. There have always been those who feel that the brother was also a creative figure who has never had his due. For the most persuasive of this school, Juliet Barker, Branwell was actually the family's literary pioneer.

> Just as he had always done, from the days of their childhood when he had been the innovator in their juvenile writings to the publishing of his poetry in more recent years, Branwell was the first member of his family to tread a new path, in seeing the potential of the novel as a marketable commodity, and setting about writing one for publication.

But, in thus describing Branwell's approach to the novel Barker has unconsciously put her finger on the flaw in his approach. As a poet he tells Wordsworth to stand aside, and *Blackwood's* to sack an established contributor so that he, P. B. Brontë, can show them all how it should be done. Now, with the novel, it is all quite simple, as he tells J. B. Leyland in September 1845.

> I knew that in the present state of the publishing and reading world a Novel is the most saleable article so that where ten pounds would be offered for a work the production of which would require the utmost stretch of a man's intellect – two hundred pounds would be a refused offer for three volumes

whose composition would require the smoking of a cigar and
the humming of a tune.

The presumption of this apart, it is a cash register approach to fiction
which is poles apart from his sisters' modest desire to set down life as
they see it, and in so doing perhaps acquit themselves with a little
honour among their peers. The arrogance might be venial if the
production could in anyway measure up to it. But Branwell never
completed more than one volume of his projected novel, *And the
Weary are at Rest*, the MS of which is held by the Department of
Rare Books & Special Collections at Princeton University (it received
private publication in 1924). This, as might be expected, is closely
based upon his affair with Mrs Robinson. But this is not the gravamen
against it. Its married heroine contemplates the contrast between her
would-be lover and her husband:

> Mrs Maria Thurston had known enough of Sorrow, and God
> had intended her to both know and feel enough of love. She
> had before her a man capable of exciting every feeling that a
> woman can know – she had, as the possessor of her own person,
> a man, if I can write him down as such, who could not gain
> more than momentarily her feelings, and who could never feel
> hers at all …

The degree of self-identification (and self-flattery) militates against
this being art on any level. Imagination is in thrall to the fevered
fancy of Branwell's Angria scribblings, from which Charlotte was
mercifully rescued by Heger. And when Mrs Thurston eventually
succumbs to her hero, she indulges in an orgy of remorse such as
Branwell wanted Mrs Robinson to feel – deluded himself that she did
feel:

> O God forgive me if thou can'st! I do not know how I have
> angered thee – I do not know whether I sin in daring to pray to
> thee – I only know that I cannot help myself, that I am going
> whither my every feeling leads me …

It can be seen at a glance that the perpetrator of this could never conceivably have matured to take his place as a novelist alongside his sisters.

Branwell's extant verse tells the same story. Yes, he was the first of the siblings to publish – hardly surprising since he was older than the two true poets among his sisters, and, as a man about town, could make the necessary contacts among the editors of local journals. Before their *Poems* appeared in 1846 he had already had a dozen or so poems printed under the pseudonym "Northangerland" in the *Halifax Guardian,* and "The Afghan War", surprisingly the only poem to appear under his own name, in the *Leeds Intelligencer.*

His poems can be experienced in the mass alongside those of the weakest contender for poetic honours among his sisters, in the Shakespeare Head Brontë volume of 1934 which is devoted to his and Charlotte's verse. It is safe to say that they do not survive even that least taxing of comparisons. While Charlotte is generally content to operate within her limitations, Branwell prefers the 'big' occasion. There is a cloying bombast about his poems. We drown in them long before we have elicited any specific meaning. Even in a subject like "Thermopylae", which from his classical education he was well qualified to bring to life, there is a complete absence of narrative gift.

Elsewhere he occasionally chooses to wear, as it were, the mantle of verse leader writer for some stalwartly conservative Yorkshire newspaper. A specimen from the jingoistic "The Afghan War" will serve to illustrate the point.

> England rise! Thine ancient thunder
> Humbled mightier foes than these;
> Broke a whole world's bonds asunder,
> Gave thee empire o'er the seas:

Even if we grant that this is occasional verse, it is dreadfully poor stuff of the type. When Branwell attempts personal feeling, the results are no better. "Juan Fernandez" and "Penmaenmawr" celebrate his hopeless love for Mrs Robinson. But even had she seen the latter in the *Halifax Guardian* it seems extremely doubtful that, as Juliet Barker asserts, "these lines must have caused her great alarm". In "Penmaenmawr", addressed to the mountain in North Wales which sets off Branwell's train of thought, there is much in the way of orology, myth, history, geology, geography and sheer bad weather to be negotiated before the beloved alights on any reference to the grand passion of which she is the presiding muse. The lady would have had to be a literary critic of more than usual stamina – and partiality – to have found anything to alarm her here.

It would occupy too much space to no profit to prove the case by quoting extensively from these longish poems. A few lines from "Epistle from a Father to a Child in her Grave" best illustrate Branwell's inability to project himself emotionally onto the circumstances of another. The lines may or may not have been his reflections on hearing of the death of an illegitimate child he had sired. It does not greatly matter.

> I write to thee what thou wilt never read,
> For heed me thou *wilt* not, howe'er may bleed
> The heart that many think a worthless stone,
> But which oft aches for some beloved one;

Real or imagined, the poignancy of the situation eludes Branwell. There is no sense of the loss of what might have been. Instead, the death of the child is immediately submerged under the poet's tender regard for his own bleeding and much mistaken heart.

There is no need to labour the point. It merely seems fair that those claims that are made for Branwell – even if they are only claims of unfulfilled potential – are at least fairly tested. And the evidence is that he was simply not equipped to be a creative writer, as we understand the term in the case of Charlotte, Emily and Anne.

Only in the sphere of translation can Branwell lay any claim to a niche in literary history. His versions of some of Horace's *Odes*, completed by 1840, bear comparison with the best of their type. They were not published until 1938. They can be enjoyed by the general reader alongside other translations, ranging from the 17th century to the present day, in the excellent paperback Wordsworth Classics edition of the *Odes,* edited by Antony Lentin and published in 1996. The year 1848 opened with the lives of the three sisters transformed. Even in those days before the modern publicity machine and speed-of-light communications, literary reputations spread like wildfire. From utter obscurity, Currer, Ellis and Action Bell found themselves on a pinnacle of fame. Literary London wanted to know who they were. It seems extraordinary, now, that Smith, Elder seemed not to mind who they were, even in the face of the mounting evidence that the 'brothers' were in fact women, provided that Currer was happy writing books for them. Thus, the cumbersome device by which Charlotte told them to keep sending 'Currer's' correspondence to her, care of Haworth parsonage, was sustained for so long.

The sisters were in no mood simply to sit back and savour this newfound celebrity. Anne was already at work on a new novel. So (it would seem from the not totally conclusive evidence of a letter from T. C. Newby) was Emily. By March 1848 *Jane Eyre* was already into its third impression. In June, Anne published *The Tenant of Wildfell Hall* (to reviews of a severity unexampled even in the vigorous reactions to *Wuthering Heights*). One might add that Patrick, by now over seventy, had made a remarkable recovery from his cataract operation and was active writing letters to various authorities and private individuals on topics ranging from the use of ether as an anaesthetic to ways of improving the performance of British small arms and artillery.

Charlotte had temporarily become creatively dormant. She had attempted a number of starts to a successor to *Jane Eyre*, but discarded them all. The fact is that she had her mental hands full with the details of what these days would be called the promotional aspect of the Brontës' success. And, suddenly, the question of the identity of the 'Brothers Bell' became a pressing problem. Newby had sought to cash in on the runaway success of *Jane Eyre* in America. He had put it about that the three Bells were one and the same person, with an eye, of course, to driving up the transatlantic sales of *Wuthering Heights* and *Agnes Grey* and securing any subsequent books by Currer Bell for the American end of his operation. In London, Smith, Elder wrote glacially to Charlotte to ask her, in plain terms, what the Bells were playing at.

As she so often did in the big matters, Charlotte acted immediately. Commandeering Anne (Emily would not be budged), she made her pack, sent their trunks on ahead, walked with her the four miles to Keighley through a summer storm which drenched them both to the skin, and, in this sodden state, boarded the night train to London.

Next day in his Cornhill offices Smith, Elder's young proprietor was astonished to be buttonholed by two wan and bedraggled women of uncertain age and outlandish garb, who claimed to be two-thirds of the by now notorious writing trio of Bell brothers. Once explanations had made all clear, Smith reacted with great urbanity. In the few days that Charlotte and Anne were in town he arranged visits to the opera, the National Gallery, the Royal Academy and to his family for the upcountry pair.

More important, Charlotte's impetuous initiative was the beginning of a close relationship with her publishers: Smith himself; William Smith Williams, the firm's perceptive and elderly reader; and the general manager, James Taylor. She never got to like London. Its brilliant coteries never afterwards filled the emotional void left by her sisters' deaths. But she added Smith and his colleagues to the small list of her genuine friends. And the relationships she had with them, frank and easy, intellectual and philosophical, and at moments something warmer than that, were a partial balm to a soul which, as it had done in Brussels, always desired to worship at altars. But the visit did not change the Brontës relationship with their public. To their readers they continued to be Currer, Ellis and Acton Bell.

Though at that moment none of them could know it, that July visit to London was to be the apogee of their collective happiness. Within nine months The Brontë family had been decimated.

Branwell was the first to die. By that time his descent into alcohol and drug addiction had become well nigh impossible to cope with. By day he might make clandestine attempts to procure another few penn'orth of gin. But that could not stave off the horrors of the night, with its screaming nerve endings and uncontrollably shaking limbs. Charlotte, by now sunk in something approaching contempt for a once-loved brother who had squandered such gifts and such opportunities, could not bear it. Only Emily had the physical and moral strength to face the grisly details of such a dissolution, unflinchingly changing fouled bedclothes and on one occasion ripping from Branwell's body sheets which he had accidentally set on fire.

He died in the evening of 24th September 1848. Chronic Bronchitis and Marasmus (the latter a meaningless term signifying 'wasting') were given as the causes of his death. A retrospective attempt by some biographers to ascribe these conditions to a far-advanced tuberculosis must be dismissed as a well-meant fiction.

Within three months Emily had followed her brother. Her death has been recorded by successive biographers lovingly and lugubriously. At what point she agreed to see a doctor; whether she died upstairs in bed or downstairs in the parlour: whether or not she failed to recognise a sprig of the heather that meant so much to her, even when it was passed in front of her eyes, are details that can be argued over indefinitely and need not concern us. In dying, as in life, she was determined to trouble no one else with her affairs. And what is perhaps more awful to consider is that this, above all her sisters, powerful constitution should decline so rapidly from the "cold & cough" which Charlotte mentions *en passant* in a letter to Ellen on 9th October 1848, to her death from tuberculosis on 21st December that same year. It is a terrible reminder of the short lease on which people held their lives in those days. Months later, in her continuing anguish for the loss of her sister's powerful and sustaining spirit, Charlotte was to cry out: "I could hardly let Emily go – I wanted to hold her back then – and I want her back now …"

The third blow was to follow not long afterwards. Anne's health was by this time causing concern. By early in the New Year consumption had been diagnosed by a medical man Patrick Brontë had brought in specially from Leeds to examine her. The disease made rapid advances, if only slightly less rapid than the 'galloping' consumption that had carried off Emily. Anne had always wanted to visit Scarborough. In May, ill though she by now was, she insisted on having her last wish, and travelled there in the company of Charlotte and Ellen Nussey, visiting York Minster on the way.

Almost the last view we have of her is an excursion in a donkey cart along the sands at Scarborough where "lest the poor donkey be urged by its driver to a greater speed than her tender heart thought right, she took the reins, and drove herself". This was on 26th May 1849. Two days later, she was dead. She is buried in Scarborough, the only one of the Brontës not to have found a final resting place at Haworth.

At her father's insistence Charlotte agreed, for the sake of her health, to continue for some weeks longer her holiday with Ellen on the drier and more salubrious East side of Yorkshire. When she returned home in June it was to a house so wrung dry with mourning that there was no room for further demonstrations of grief. She and her father greeted each other with that understated, merely cordial, affection which families often use to support each other, in moments of unutterable sorrow.

After her father and the servants had retired for the night, Charlotte was left in the parlour with her own thoughts once more. It is almost unendurably painful to contemplate the sole survivor of that creative sisterhood, pacing alone, now, at nights in that same room where they had shared so freely of each others' hopes for the future.

In a letter to William Smith Williams, she powerfully describes her sense of desolation:

A year ago – had a prophet warned me how I should stand in June 1849 – how stripped and bereaved – had he foretold the autumn, the winter, the spring of sickness and suffering to be gone through – I should have thought – this can never be endured. It is over. Branwell – Emily – Anne are gone like dreams – gone as Maria and Elizabeth went twenty years ago. One by one I have watched them fall asleep on my arm – and closed their glazed eyes ...

The least equipped of the three to sustain such a lonely state, endure she nevertheless must. She picked up the work she had begun before the terminal illnesses of her sisters had taken over her mental preoccupations, the novel which was to become in due course *Shirley*. In a moment of self doubt, she had, even before the death of Anne, sent the tentative first volume to Smith, Elder and invited their comments. Smith, Smith Williams and Taylor (who although on the managerial side in the firm was admitted to editorial deliberations) conferred on the single volume and admitted to some quite serious reservations. But they toned down their critique when passing it on to Charlotte. Realising that their author was passing through one of the supreme crises of her life, they murmured their reservations as a codicil to their general approval.

Taylor himself made the journey to Haworth to collect the final MS of *Shirley* from her in September 1849. It was published in the following month. Ironically, given Smith, Elder's reservations about the coarseness of the opening scenes, which depict country curates as something less than spiritually admirable, the novel was a great hit in Yorkshire with the very people it lampooned. Several local clerics gloried in their fictional identities and took to styling themselves to each other in their *Shirley* personae rather than by their real names. One of these, Haworth's assistant curate from Ireland, the Rev Arthur Bell Nicholls, read out Charlotte's liveliest scenes to the Rev Patrick Brontë, revelling in the unsparing treatment of himself.

Shirley was different enough in atmosphere from *Jane Eyre* to garner a clutch of reviews which were kindly enough not to discourage

Charlotte. The reservations expressed were on the score of her handling of her material. *The Times* praised her "faculty of graphic description, the strong imagination, the fervid and masculine diction, the analytical skill," but went on to observe that these qualities "are thrown away on a structure that bears no relation to actual life". G. H. Lewes, who reviewed the novel in the *Edinburgh Review,* accused her characters of exhibiting "intolerable rudeness of manner, and observed acutely that "The various scenes are gathered up into three volumes – they have not grown into a work." But there was no full blooded onslaught on the moral character of the author of the sort which had been launched on Emily and Anne. The sheer level of interest in a new work from the author of *Jane Eyre* was immense, and was enough to insure against an outright critical dismissal.

Interest in the work and in its author were now inseparable. In the winter of 1849 Charlotte paid her second visit to London and met Thackeray and the fashionable religious and social writer Harriet Martineau. Lionisation was becoming inescapable. When she returned home, a Lancashire baronet, Sir James Kay Shuttleworth, suddenly aware that he had a 'hot' literary property living close by in a neighbouring county, tried to take her up and whirl her to London to show her off to his circle. Illness on both sides forestalled this and in May 1850, she gratefully accepted a second invitation from George Smith to spend a longer period of time with him and his mother at their Gloucester Terrace home. Here, at least, she escaped the worst terrors of the exploitation Kay Shuttleworth had in mind for her. A bonus, however, of the Kay Shuttleworths' repeated attentions to her was that through them Charlotte met Mrs Gaskell, with whom she established an instant rapport. It was a meeting of two minds which had been weaned on the social strife of the industrial North, at a far remove from the salons of the metropolitan South.

Her greatest torments came from meeting those she admired. In the company of her idol Thackeray, urbane and sparkling with cynical wit, her genius was rebuked. "… with him I was fearfully stupid," she reported back to Ellen. Shrinking into herself in these brilliant literary gatherings, she would sit in a corner of the room, inclining her head at a tangent even to those she found the courage to speak to. G. H. Lewes gives us a penetrating glimpse of her: "a little plain, provincial, sickly-looking old maid," in a comment to George Eliot, but adds "yet what passion, what fire in her!"

For a woman of Charlotte's acute sensitivities Smith, Elder proved ideal publishers. They swallowed whatever degree of disappointment they may have felt over the quality of *Shirley,* and waited patiently for its successor, *Villette.* It was eventually published in January 1853 to reviews which on the whole did it justice by estimating its merits as lying somewhere between those of *Jane Eyre* and *Shirley.* That estimate has, by and large, stood the test of time.

But, additionally for Charlotte, there was intellectual intimacy, not to say emotional excitement, in her relationship with the principal men of Smith, Elder. William Smith Williams had, from the first, shown himself a wise counsellor to Charlotte in her extremities of grief. But, notwithstanding their mental affinity, his being married ruled out his being any more than that. George Smith, talented, handsome and eight years younger than her, was a different matter. It is clear from the skittish tone of her letters to him, that she was attracted to him. Early on in their association there seems to have been a strongish predilection for her on his part. When in the summer of 1850 he had to go to Scotland to bring a young brother home from his boarding school, he insisted, to the horror of his mother, that Charlotte go with him. There is something far from ingenuous in Charlotte's laughing disclaimer to Ellen of any impropriety in such an arrangement.

> Now I believe that George and I understand each other very well – and respect each other very sincerely – we both know the wide breach time has made between us – we do not embarrass each other, or very rarely – my six or eight years of seniority, to say nothing of lack of all pretension to beauty &c. are a perfect safeguard – I should not in the least fear to go

with him to China – I like to see him pleased – I greatly dislike
to ruffle and disappoint him – so he shall have his mind ...

The lady doth protest too much we think. The careless use of the
Christian name to a third party is telling. The relationship implied by
her insistence on deference to Smith's humours has already gone
beyond anything conceivably required between publisher and author.
The masochism always latent in Charlotte is surfacing again. There
are strange echoes of the fictional Jane Eyre/St John Rivers episode
in the reference to going to China. In letters to Smith himself, the
tone becomes undisguisedly warmer, as time progresses.

> Can I help wishing you well when I owe you, directly or
> indirectly, most of the good moments I now enjoy? . . . You do
> not know – you cannot know how strongly his [i.e. Currer Bell's
> – she now playfully switches to her authorial persona] nature
> inclines him to adopt suggestions coming from so friendly a
> quarter . . .

And there is icy formality in her reaction, in December 1853, to the
news that he has become engaged to another.

> My dear Sir,
> In great happiness, as in great grief – words of sympathy
> should be few. Accept my meed of congratulation – and
> believe me
>
> Sincerely yours
> C. Brontë

To be fair to Charlotte, this is not simply the reaction of an
embittered spinster. Even at this stage of her life, she did not lack
romantic attentions. She had before this turned down two proposals
of marriage, one in March 1851 from Smith, Elder's office manager,
James Taylor, and a second, in December 1852, from her father's
curate, Arthur Bell Nicholls. But where she gave her heart, she gave
it all.

Whatever it was that Arthur Bell Nicholls eventually secured in April 1854, with Charlotte's consent to marry him, it was certainly not her heart. To Ellen she wrote on 11th April:

> I believe him to be an affectionate – a conscientious – a high principled man – and if with all this, I should yield to regrets – that fine talents, congenial tastes and thoughts are not added – it seems to me I should be most presumptuous and thankless.

To do him credit – and beyond this point in the story one is not inclined to give him much of that – in the period of his courtship Bell seems to have been in love with Charlotte in the best head-over-heels tradition. Having at first despaired of her hand, he applied for that time-honoured panacea to thwarted clerical love, missionary work in the Antipodes. (Her father was violently opposed to Bell, having perhaps thought of grander liaisons for his now famous daughter – he had been enthusiastic over the Taylor suit, when the Smith, Elder manager had presented himself at Haworth.)

Yet, having once married Charlotte, Bell behaved with the perfect complacency of the average Victorian husband, gently but insistently trying to bully her out of everything that made her what she was. (He was not always successful: on her honeymoon she insisted on being left alone on a clifftop to savour the fury of the Atlantic Ocean by herself; and back at Haworth, she began her unfinished fragment *Emma.*)

By contrast, her esteem for him, having started at zero on the Richter scale of love, seems to have grown quite rapidly. The novelty of sexual intimacy must have had something to do with this. At least he cannot have been an insensitive brute in bed. Her ardent nature would have recoiled from that. And she could hardly have refrained from leaking some hint of disappointment over shortcomings in that department to Ellen, to whom, as we have seen, she was allowed to continue writing uncensored by her husband.

Yet marriage killed her. It is difficult to judge such things by standards of today. Men married, bedded and simply let the consequences run their course. Yet one cannot help succumbing to anger over the complacent recklessness of behaviour like Bell's, which could impregnate a manifestly frail, chronically ill and, by the standards of the day, over-aged woman like Charlotte, and then sit back and watch her die.

She was thirty eight. We must, I suppose, keep before us the thought that pregnancy at any age was potentially life-threatening in those days. But Mr Brontë had it right at the outset when he said that he thought Charlotte "was not strong enough for marriage".

So, on 31st March 1855, died the last of these gifted and great-souled women. She was three months pregnant. In her case morning sickness had developed into

> nights indescribable – sickness with scarce a reprieve – I strain
> until what I vomit is mixed with blood.

This is a recognisable description of *hyperemesis gravidarum*. In a nature like Charlotte's it may well have been psychogenic in origin. But whether psychogenic or not, it could certainly have been treated today. Charlotte's description of it, in a letter to Amelia Taylor, wife of Mary Taylor's brother Joe, was probably the last thing she wrote on this earth.

Patrick buried the last of his daughters. Never in good health, he was nevertheless to outlive her by six years, dying on 7th June 1861 at the age of 88. After his death Arthur Bell Nicholls returned to Ireland, to Banagher, close to the Leinster-Connaught border, where he had been brought up by an uncle, Dr Bell. There, he settled with his aunt. In 1864 he married his cousin Mary Bell. A childless marriage, it nevertheless appears to have been a companionable one. The second Mrs Nicholls had the good sense to cope with the burgeoning myth of her predecessor. And by his retreat to Ireland, Nicholls ensured that she was not exposed to the worst excesses of Brontë worship which, within a few years of Charlotte's death, were already making Haworth a place of pilgrimage.

He died in Banagher in December 1906 at the age of 87. His wife survived him for another eight years, dying in February 1915.

6 CHARLOTTE BRONTË: *JANE EYRE*

WERE we to conform to the chronology of Charlotte Brontë's creative life, *The Professor* would have to be the starting point. But it was published after her death, in 1857, and reads so obviously like a trial run for *Villette* that it makes no sense to consider it among her major works. Though it has undeniable strengths, it will always seem to be an appendage to her *oeuvre*. Hailed in its day as the supreme Brontë achievement, *Jane Eyre* went into partial eclipse (with the critics, that is: it has never lost its popularity) with the opening of the 20th century, and the development of a strong lobby for the competing claims of *Wuthering Heights*. In the last few decades this balance has been redressed. Since the 1970s a new school of feminist commentators has rehabilitated Jane, exonerated Charlotte Brontë from the charge of Gothic melodrama, and furnished an analysis of every phase of the novel which finds unassailable artistic and moral logic in the final union of Jane with the maimed Rochester. From this analysis Jane Eyre emerges as the pioneering feminist heroine of her times.

There is something in such a view. What astonished contemporary reviewers, the bold fury with which this young protagonist confronts her oppressors in the early part of the book, strikes us, too, with undiminished power. Jane's predicament excites moral indignation and pity in a way unsurpassed even by Dickens at his most persuasive. It is in her relations with Rochester that unease comes in. (And to say this is to place a pretty large question mark against the moral coherence of the novel.) Is she really, in this relationship, the exemplar, as Adrienne Rich sees it, of "Charlotte Brontë's feminist manifesto?" Or is Rochester, as Leslie Stephen put it, "the personification of a true women's longing (may one say it now?) for a strong master". Incidentally, 'now' in Stephen's case is 1877, not far short of a century before Adrienne Rich's opinion was delivered.

The most powerful part of *Jane Eyre* is its opening section. In spite of indignation which often burns at white heat, Charlotte Brontë is in total control of her material The book's opening is masterly.

> There was no possibility of a walk that day. We had been
> wandering, indeed, in the leafless shrubbery an hour in the
> morning; but since dinner (Mrs Reed, when there was no
> company, dined early) the cold winter had brought with it clouds
> so sombre, and a rain so penetrating, that further outdoor
> exercise was out of the question.

In a handful of sentences the scene is set. Outdoor life in the hill country of the North West of England, where winters dominate the memory and summers are brief, is a hostile environment to young persons who cannot afford to be well wrapped up. Yet, in a very few more sentences we learn that an even worse hell awaits Jane indoors. Before the first chapter is out we understand that she is orphaned, despised and subject to the caprices and whims of her adoptive family. She is scorned by the aunt who was enjoined by her dying brother to care for her. The family servants, though perhaps secretly sympathising, dumbly echo the meaningless "moral" strictures which are daily levelled at her. She is physically bullied by that waking terror of the tiny (and especially girl) child, an overweight, indulged boy who has unthinking parental sanction for the most outrageous exercise of his power over her. When she turns on him in righteous rage she is punished in a manner which drives her to the brink of insanity. Charlotte Brontë here understands tyranny and evokes the cruelties of unopposed, arbitrary power as surely as if she had done time in a Soviet gulag.

There is perhaps no more exhilarating scene in the English novel than the moment in which Jane rebels against all this in a manner which – if only momentarily, so it seems – does at last confound her tormentors.

> "I am glad you are no relation of mine: I will never call you
> aunt again so long as I live. I will never come to see you when
> I am grown up; and if anyone asks me how I liked you, and

how you treated me, I will say the very thought of you makes
me sick, and that you treated me with miserable cruelty."

There is nothing remotely feminist about this. It is the outrage every bullied child has felt, at that moment in which there is nothing to do but revolt, even though he/she knows the rebellion will only bring more arbitrary chastisement.

What provokes this outburst is Jane's first meeting with Mr Brocklehurst, the proprietor of the school for which she is destined. To Jane the idea of school is at first a godsend. It will be miraculous release from what she endures in the house of her aunt Reed. But the notion is turned to gall almost before it is proposed. She hears her aunt traduce her character before Brocklehurst. She knows that this new phase of her life, too, will begin under a cloud. The desire of the child to be liked – at least approved of – is again trampled down.

Whether or not Brocklehurst is an accurate or even just portrait of the Rev William Carus Wilson of Cowan Bridge need not concern us. The point is that he is a recognisably cruel, pharisaical nature of a type that occurs in all ages. According to Sandra Gilbert (whose study *The Madwoman in the Attic,* co-written with Susan Gubar, is the defining feminist text in *Jane Eyre* studies):

> As many readers have noticed, this personification of the Victorian superego is – like St John Rivers, his counterpart in the last third of the book – consistently described in phallic terms: he is a "black pillar" with a grim face at the top… like a carved mask" almost as if he were a funereal and oddly Freudian piece of furniture."

This is sheer nonsense. Even if it were sustainable from the text, why should an eight or nine-year-old girl be immediately thinking of Brocklehurst in phallic terms? What have a "black pillar" and a "carved mask" to do with the penis? What on earth does "funereal and oddly Freudian" mean? And, finally to dispose of Ms Gilbert's arguments, St John Rivers is not in any way a counterpart of Brocklehurst, who has no influence on her, but of Rochester, who does; both are men she is disposed to worship.

Jane is quite explicit about the source of her anguish in her encounter with Brocklehurst. It is that anguish of helplessness, of what Dr Johnson, in another context, called "that deferred hope that makes the heart sick" that will be recognised by any child, without recourse to Freud.

> Well might I dread, well might I dislike Mrs Reed; for it was her nature to wound me cruelly ... however carefully I obeyed, however strenuously I strove to please her my efforts were still repulsed and repaid by sentences such as the above. Now, uttered before a stranger, the accusation [i.e. that she is deceitful] cut me to the heart; I dimly perceived that she was already obliterating hope from the new phase of existence which she destined me to enter; I felt, though I could not have expressed the feeling, that she was sowing aversion and unkindness along my future path ...

At Lowood school, where Jane is now transplanted, the torment continues. There is a wonderful evocation of the utter dread a child feels of being humiliated in front of its peers. Brocklehurst has come on a school inspection. No trivium of organisation is beneath his impertinent notice: strict economies are to be practised in the issue of darning needles; (but, at the same time) why are the girls' stockings not in a better state of repair? (He has been inspecting the underwear on the washing line: now there *is* something Freudian in this that Ms Gilbert might have addressed herself to.); why was an extra ration of bread and cheese served last week?; why is one pupil of the girls wearing curls? &c., &c. As this impertinent inquisition of the school's headmistress continues, Jane, cowering at the back of the class, fervently hopes to escape detection. But her nerves betray her and she drops her slate. Brocklehurst recognises her and recollects that he had promised her aunt to expose Jane's supposed character for deceit before the whole school. She is ordered to the front of the class.

> Of my own accord I could not have stirred; I was paralysed:
> but the two great girls who sat on each side of me, set me on
> my legs and pushed me towards the dread judge.

The psychosomatic effects of Jane's agony of apprehension are acutely observed. It is terror as only a child can know it and, like Charlotte Brontë, we cannot help shaking our fist at its perpetrator. Jane is now subjected to an analysis of her character which, of course, bears no relation to reality.

But from here on, at least, she has partners in misfortune, among whom may be counted the headmistress of Lowood, Miss Temple. Jane gradually attains to a degree of self respect, and it is external enemies such as disease, which become the greatest threat to continued existence at the school. The death of the forbearing Helen Burns, cradled in Jane's arms, is poignant without toppling over into sentimentality.

To this point, quite apart from its castigation of some of the social injustices of the time – which undoubtedly include the plight of women, whether as the children of families of modest means, or as young adults who have to overcome this disadvantage – *Jane Eyre's* most potent single characteristic is its passionate belief in the sanctity of the self. And it was undoubtedly the nakedness of the manner in which this was opposed to the behests of the Victorian God, which appalled its critics.

Once Jane leaves Lowood to seek a living in the outside world, the book somehow changes gear. Put simply, the transition is from social novel to Gothic romance. From the outset, the very proximity of Rochester seems to open the Gothic windows in Jane's imagination. Her first glimpse of him is on a winter's evening. She hears his horse approaching her up a narrow lane. In her fancy the animal is momentarily translated into a 'Gytrash', a spirit in animal form which haunts Northern wildernesses.

Rochester proves himself mere flesh and blood when his horse falls on the ice. But from the outset, as Jane goes to help him, a mystery is established round his character. More important for Jane, and the dynamics of her relationship with the world around her – a world in which, to that point, she has earned the right to live on equal terms – the master/servant relationship is established between them. The world for Jane is never to be the same again. Only a few pages earlier she had been soliloquising:

Nobody knows how many rebellions besides political rebellions ferment in the masses of life which people earth. Women are supposed to be very calm generally: but women feel just as men feel; they need exercise for their faculties and a field for their efforts as much as their brothers do; they suffer from too rigid a restraint, too absolute a stagnation, precisely as men would suffer; and it is narrow-minded in their more privileged fellow creatures to say that they ought to confine themselves by making puddings and knitting stockings …

From the moment she becomes acquainted with Rochester, Jane's feminist manifesto goes into abeyance. The focus of the book is narrowed to: Will she, the governess without rank or fortune, succeed, for all her mental endowments, in captivating her 'master'? And – freely to acknowledge the skill with which Charlotte Brontë works this transition in the novel – that becomes the reader's burning preoccupation also. Within a very few pages of the beginning of the mental fencing between the pair which ends in their loving each other, we have forgotten all about the sufferings of the child Jane, and the social injustice and hypocrisy with which the underprivileged are treated. These issues have become subsumed in the burning question: will Jane 'get' Rochester?

This makes for fine romantic drama. But is it not fatal to the integrity of the book as psychological study of (what is after all) a sexual relationship?

Jane falls in love with Rochester, so we are to understand, because he forms a genuine estimate of her qualities against the flashier, competing claims of other candidates for his notice, personified by Blanche Ingram. But, for all that, is he any more 'real' as a man than say Jane Austen's Darcy, who does precisely the same thing vis-à-vis

Elizabeth Bennet? Is Rochester, indeed, as *real* as Darcy, who when he comes wooing for Elizabeth after his first rebuff, does so in an accession of genuine humility; he is without the boastful archness Jane has, to the end, to submit to from Rochester.

It seems to me that the very entrance of Rochester and the world he brings in his wake – a lurid past, a lovechild – introduces into *Jane Eyre* something that is not only foreign to Charlotte Brontë's experience but alien to her sympathies. Even before Rochester's appearance the tone is set by Adèle, the mysterious French ward to whom Jane has been chosen as governess. She is a mere cipher: a doll – and a foreign doll at that. She is the butt of Charlotte's deep-seated prejudice against Continentals – especially if they happen to be Catholic Continentals. Adèle's lisping French offers a diversion to the fact that her creator cannot be interested in her as an individual. Although she always disclaimed any liking for children in her life, Charlotte Brontë can, as we have already seen in the earlier phases of *Jane Eyre,* sympathise deeply with their feelings.

As the daughter of a French opera dancer who, we learn, has abandoned her to "the slime and mud of Paris", Adèle has doubtless not had a very stable childhood, for all that it may have been lived in an atmosphere a few degrees Celsius above that of Jane's. But Charlotte Brontë is in no mood to expend any imaginative sympathy on her case. When, to prepare herself for one of the Thornfield festive evenings, the child begs a flower "seulement pour compléter ma toilette," Jane replies with Brocklehurstian primness:

> "You think too much of your 'toilette', Adèle: but you may have a flower." And I took a rose from a vase and fastened it to her sash. She sighed a sigh of ineffable satisfaction, as if her cup of happiness were now full. I turned my face away to conceal a smile I could not suppress: there was something ludicrous as well as painful in the little Parisienne's earnest and innate devotion to matters of dress.

Jane's dismissal of this scrap of humanity nobody wants is as out-of-hand as that of the man who may, or may not, be her father. To

Rochester, too, Adèle is simply a bauble.

But there are more serious objections to what one may term the suspension of Jane's critical faculties as soon as Rochester comes within the ambit of her life. She – and we – are flattered by his interest in those of her mental and moral characteristics which we, too, are disposed to admire. Here is a man, we say, who can esteem courage and independence of mind, whatever unpromising exterior they are housed in. What we are in danger of not perceiving – as indeed she does not – is that his whole approach to her is in fact a calculated flirtation.

From the outset of their association she allows him to assume the mantle of Othello to her Desdemona. His conveniently generalised, supposedly lurid, past imposes on her credulity as surely as the Moor's "Anthropophagi, and men whose heads/Do grow beneath their shoulders" do on Brabantio's daughter. It is a past without real substance because it is a past beyond Charlotte Brontë's experience. His tale of his betrayal by Adèle's mother, Céline Varens, is plucked from the stock of such betrayal stories. Neither Céline, nor her new lover, nor the betrayed Rochester have any real, in the sense of being specific, existence as this account unfolds. And when Rochester patronises her for her lack of experience of life:

> "You think all existence lapses in as quiet a flow as that in which your youth has hitherto slid away. Floating on with closed eyes and muffled ears, you neither see the rocks bristling not far off in the bed of the flood, not hear the breakers boil at their base."

we long for her tartly to remind him that she has known deprivation, want, and physical and mental agony, by the side of which a wealthy young man's miscued flirtation with a ballet girl is commonplace. But she doesn't. Instead, she hears out his story to the end and, later, in the quiet of her own room comes to this conclusion about the narrator:

> I believed he was naturally a man of better tendencies, higher
> principles, and purer tastes than such as circumstances had
> developed, education instilled, or destiny encouraged. I thought
> there were excellent materials in him, though for the present
> they hung together somewhat spoiled and tangled.

Alas, this is self-delusion on no more exalted a level than that of an East End bride who might fondly imagine (and most would not) that after their marriage her man will give up his football supporter's scarf, his rattler and his weekly visit to Upton Park. (One might add, *en passant,* that as a bad man, with a bad past, and every intention of behaving badly after his wedding day, Anne Brontë's Arthur Huntingdon has a reality which is never achieved by Rochester.)

Once embarked on, Jane's course of willing suspension of disbelief is fatal to her capacity to form a true estimate of what Rochester is, and what is going on at Thornfield. When his wife Bertha Mason escapes from her quarters and sets fire to him the "surges of joy" (her words) she feels at having been able to act as his "cherished preserver" (his) occupy her later reflections to the detriment of any suspicions she might harbour. And this is notwithstanding that the fire is a manifestly suspicious business and that the figure of the top storey servant Grace Poole is beginning to assume highly sinister proportions. Already, her psychological dependence on Rochester is much further advanced than Jane realises. It is patent in the terms in which she tries to banish her suspicions of Grace Poole from her mind. She has been nursing some idea that the servant may, perhaps, have some mysterious power over Rochester (which, in a way, she has).

> I hastened to drive from my mind the hateful notion I had been
> conceiving respecting Grace Poole; it disgusted me. I compared
> myself with her, and found we were different. Bessie Leaven
> had said I was quite a lady; and she spoke truth – I was a lady.
> And now I looked much better than I did when Bessie saw me;
> I had more colour and more flesh, more life, more vivacity,
> because I had brighter hopes and keener enjoyments.

We cannot help feeling keenly that the brave Jane who outfaced Aunt Reed and Mr Brocklehurst from the ground of her own merits and the conviction of her rectitude has gone a long way down the path of compromise with the world of appearances to have to prefer herself to Grace Poole on the score that she is now a lady – and, at that, a lady conscious of the strong approval of a gentleman of substance.

Rochester now sets himself to toy with Jane's affections. Indeed, what happens next seems to me to raise questions against his conduct and intentions which are little less fundamental than those later posed by his attempt to trap her into a bigamous marriage. In terms of the suspense we expect from a love story, Rochester's apparent transference of his attentions from Jane to Blanche Ingram, of titled but impecunious family, is doubtless in some way acceptable. But what actually lies behind it?

Throughout her association with him, Miss Ingram demonstrates at every turn that she is a heartless snob who could not possibly make Rochester the soulmate he allegedly craves. Why, then, does Charlotte Brontë subject us to the insultingly crude mechanical device by which he claims to come a conviction of Jane's superior merits?

> "Little sceptic [he tells Jane], you *shall* be convinced. What love have I for Miss Ingram? None: and that you know. What love has she for me? None: as I have taken pains to prove: I caused a rumour to reach her that my fortune was not a third of what was supposed, and after that I presented myself to see the results; it was coldness both from her and her mother. I would not – I could not – marry Miss Ingram."

After which he condescends to offer himself to the "poor and obscure, and small and plain" Jane. But suppose Miss Ingram *had* thought a third of whatever Rochester was supposed to be worth was better than being left on the shelf? Are we to suppose he would have accepted her? Was it only the degree of Blanche's mercenary expectations that ruled her out? Her failure to pass the "one third of supposed estate" test is surely not a resolution which leaves Jane with much self respect.

Yet the feminist Sandra Gilbert is able to entertain the following roseate view of Rochester's decision to propose to Jane:

> Brontë appears here to have imagined a world in which the prince and Cinderella are democratically equal... master and servant are profoundly alike. And to the marriage of true minds, it seems, no man or woman can admit impediment.

an analysis which has to negotiate mountains of scepticism on our part.

Amid multiplying evidence that all is not well at Thornfield, Jane sleepwalks towards her marriage. At moments she surfaces from a state of happy self-delusion to assert herself in the old way. She resists Rochester's attempts to dress her up in finery, as he did his Céline, with spirit and sense. She is sceptical about the most violent of his protestations.

> "I suppose your love will effervesce in six months, or less. I have observed in books written by men, that period assigned as the farthest to which a husband's ardour extends. Yet, after all, as a friend and companion, I hope never to become quite distasteful ..."

But to the repeated demonstrations that Rochester's past life contains some grisly secret, which culminates spectacularly in her waking in bed to find his wife trying on her, Jane's, wedding veil, she remains resolutely blind. Fortunately, Mason, severely treated by Jane as having a vacant eye (presumably intended to indicate to us the onset of his sister's madness at no great distance), comes to the rescue. The marriage service is halted in the midst by the conclusive proof that Rochester is already married, and that his (mad) wife is kept under constraint in a upper room at Thornfield.

Whether Rochester had a right to secure himself some happiness by committing a criminal act, does not, to me, seem open to discussion. He had not, and to do so by deceiving an innocent like Jane in a manner that would have destroyed her reputation for good, seems simply cowardly. But there has, all along, been something shifty and sneaking in his methods.

But that is not how Jane sees it.

> Reader, I forgave him at the moment and on the spot. There
> was such deep remorse in his eye, such true pity in his tone,
> such manly energy in his manner; and besides, there was such
> unchanged love in his whole look and mien –

We would like to be able to agree, but somehow cannot. If Rochester
had wanted to break out of his marriage trap even at the cost of flouting
conventional morality, why didn't he tell Jane what his situation was
at the outset, and ask her to be his mistress? She would have turned
him down, of course. But he would at least have been giving her the
chance to see him plain.

Once rumbled, this is what Rochester now does, but only after a
self-pitying recital of his woes. The blame for his present predicament
is placed squarely on Bertha Mason and her family. The young
Rochester had been "sent out to Jamaica, to espouse a bride already
courted for me". True, his father wants him to make his fortune thereby,
but why, like the far less courageous George Osborne of *Vanity Fair*
offered a similar opportunity, he cannot refuse to "marry that mulatto
woman", we are not told. Flattered and cajoled, Rochester finds
himself "allied to a cast of mind singularly common, low, narrow and
singularly incapable of being led to anything higher". To Jane he
accuses his lack of judgement in so consenting. But his self-reproach
is as nothing compared to the blame he reserves for others. After
their marriage his wife is revealed as an imbecile, a drunk and a
nymphomaniac. He finds himself "bound to a wife at once intemperate
and unchaste". (This is a bit rich coming from a man who has gone
through life helping himself to women as and when he pleases.) To
compound his woes, madness, kept from him until after the nuptials,
is now found to run in the family into which he has married. Bertha
soon goes mad herself – the condition brought on prematurely by her
sexual excesses.

Set down, thus, the Rochester defence of his intention to commit a crime against Jane is seen as the farrago of medical, psychological and moral nonsense it surely is. Meanwhile, equally implausibly, the "tall, dark, majestic" Miss Mason, "a fine woman in the style of Miss Blanche Ingram" (Rochester does not seem to be able to keep off that topic) and the "boast of Spanish Town for her beauty," has, as Mrs Rochester, degenerated physically into the frightful apparition, ghastly, bloated, black-faced and red-eyed, which confronted Jane on the eve of her wedding. (Would Miss Ingram have suffered a similar fate, had she had married him, one asks?)

The whole Bertha Mason past, as well as present, suffers from being inorganic to the main stream of the novel's preoccupations. It is unreal like much else in Rochester's life that we cannot actually see before us. And now, further to ingratiate himself with the pitying Jane, he regales her with a round of mistresses, indulged in to take his mind off his unhappy domestic situation – "... dissipation – never debauchery: that I hated and hate," he assures her.

By this time we cannot help wishing she would turn on her heel and leave him soliloquising to his fantastic conceit. But she does not. She stays to listen to his hectoring proposals that she become his mistress, since he has failed to make her his unlawful wife. When she declines his proposal he demands petulantly.

"Then you will not yield?"
"No."
"Then you condemn me to live wretched and to die accursed?"
"I advise you to live sinless ..."
"Then you snatch love and innocence from me? You fling me back on lust for a passion – vice for an occupation?"

There is something deeply objectionable in this – though doubtless it is no more or less than the recognisable language of moral blackmail as practised against susceptible women by cowardly men in all ages. Far from being the partnership of equals detected by Susan Gilbert, the relationship has become for Rochester purely a matter of subjecting Jane to his will. And his threat that her refusal to yield consigns him again to the life of vice (which he has only just strenuously denied indulging in) is contemptible.

Jane does not see it this way. His words cut her. She is "tortured by a sense of remorse" by his unjust, piqued and selfish accusations. When she escapes him and goes to bed, a long night of struggle awaits her before a still small voice in the darkness whispers to her:

"My daughter, flee temptation."

and she answers

"Mother, I will."

Christian conscience has won through. And with the morning, Jane is, like Bunyan's protagonist, on the way that leads through Despond, Difficulty and Humiliation, before her version of the Celestial City is gained.

After the moral dubiety inherent in life under the Thornfield roof, the penultimate phase of *Jane Eyre* returns its protagonist to purer air. But first she must undergo a brief purgatory. She has fled Rochester improvidently ill-equipped, and has jumped on a coach without the means to pay her way. She is put down by the coachman in the middle of nowhere after two days journey, when her slender stock of money runs out. After begging unsuccessfully in the locality, she almost dies of exposure before she is given succour by the Rivers family, a brother and two sisters, at their moorland home.

Her contact with them restores a moral clarity to her life. It also resurrects in the novel some of the concern for contemporary social issues Charlotte Brontë had seemed in danger of forgetting in the emotional excitement of the Thornfield menage. Through St John Rivers, the austere incumbent of Morton parish, she is given an opportunity to do social good, and thereby to rediscover her own worth. Thanks to a private benefactor, Rivers can establish a school for girls in the area. Jane agrees to be its sole mistress. The episode provides a nugget of real social interest in the way it shows how education at such an epoch and in such a place relied on the patronage of individuals. For Jane

> ... compared with that of governess in a rich house, it was
> independent; and the fear of servitude with strangers entered
> my soul like iron: it was not ignoble – not unworthy – not
> mentally degrading.

And she goes on to a sense of fulfilment from being able to impart some useful attainments to the unlettered daughters of the locality.

There is, unfortunately, a drawback. St John Rivers wants to become a missionary, and he has long since chosen Jane as his helpmeet. As a soldier of Christ he is no less importunate than Rochester was as a man of lust. Jane again comes under tremendous psychological pressure as Rivers – who cannot love her – insists that the only way she can go to India with him is as his wife. She has already given up her German studies for Hindustani, for him. She is quite prepared to serve him as his curate (she *does* seem to have a difficulty in resisting the demands of a masterful nature, be they sexual or spiritual). But the idea of marriage to him revolts her.

Nevertheless, she is teetering on the brink of even that momentous step, when Charlotte Brontë rescues her with the famous Rochester 'cry in the night'. This remarkable example of telepathy has been much discussed. With it, we abandon, once again, the psychological realism which, in *Jane Eyre,* does constant battle with fantastic and melodramatic elements. For Sandra Gilbert, Jane's

> new and apparently telepathic communication with Rochester...
> has been made possible by her new independence and by
> Rochester's new humility. The plot device of the cry is merely
> a sign that the relationship for which both lovers have always
> longed is now possible, a sign that Jane's metaphoric speech
> of the first betrothal scene has been translated into reality: "My
> spirit... addresses your spirit, just as if we had both passed
> through the grave, and we stood at God's feet, equal – as we
> are!"

But what, actually, has matured in their relationship? Jane goes in search of Rochester to find that Bertha has been conveniently eliminated and that in the process Rochester has been so severely injured and blinded that he is naturally glad to think his governess still wants him. But is he otherwise altered? Suppose Jane had answered his *cri de coeur* to find him injured, but still with wife? What could have been her proposal, and what the resolution of the novel, then?

The fact is that the dénouement represents no emotional or philosophical advance in the relationship between them. Even Rochester's comparative humility is that of the merely chastened sort. And to his sudden accession of religious feeling at the end of the book,

> "I humbly entreat my Redeemer to give me strength to lead a henceforth purer life than I have done hitherto!"

we can hardly help musing "Ah, but what if he doesn't?" A Rochester some years on, with sight and physical vigour returning, is a much less certain proposition than the biddable physical wreck Jane inherits in the last chapter.

Doubtless we are churlish to think such thoughts. Jane's ecstatic act of faith, "Reader, I married him," is meant to be the end of it. And in those terms *Jane Eyre* may be allowed to stand as the supreme romantic melodrama. But that is a very different thing from according it a place among the great psychological studies of love between man and woman in the European novel. Rochester and Jane are united by an affection which we take on trust, and by some convenient manipulation of plot by the author. They have not had to battle their way to their love by acknowledging and redeeming the defects in their own natures as, say, Pierre Besukhov and Natasha Rostov do in Tolstoy's *War and Peace*.

7 SHIRLEY

IT MAY be oversimplifying the problem of *Shirley* to observe that its eponymous heroine does not set foot in the novel until almost a third of the way through, and that the man she eventually marries does not appear until we are well into the last third of the book. But the fact is that however much we admire *Shirley* for the historical research which has gone into Charlotte Brontë's portrait of Napoleonic Wars industrial North Britain: for its array of formidably articulated ideas; for the gallery of characters she has assembled to give them expression; *Shirley* suffers fatally for its lack of focus.

It is the most difficult novel to *remember* of all the Brontë stories. We can admire Shirley at moments for her strength, her beauty, her devil-may-care approach to life, but she has no power over the imagination, and does not linger in the mind. Her creator has made her, as a wealthy mill-owner, too immune from so much of what concerns others in the novel. It is Caroline Helstone, her co-heroine and a more characteristic Charlotte protagonist: shrinking, self-doubting and loving in constant doubt of a return, with whom we sympathise. And there is something a little gratuitous in the fact that the adored Shirley must receive (and decline) a proposal of marriage from Caroline's beloved, too, before the poor thing is allowed, at last, to claim him and be happy. Shirley then selects for a husband a man who must be the least memorable consort of any heroine in English literature.

Another serious weakness of the novel is that both its women protagonists are financially independent. Shirley is rich. Caroline may want to marry, or to have a career as teacher or governess, but she has a competence and does not need to. Indeed, for all we hear of her excellence as a teacher, throughout the book, we do not observe her doing a stroke of work. This freedom from economic imperatives is something Charlotte Brontë does not really understand, and it tends to undermine her purpose. Shirley can descant on her social responsibilities; Caroline can ventilate Charlotte's favourite themes:

the woman's lot; the slavery of being a governess; as long as they like. But the latter, in particular, speaks as Charlotte Brontë and not as Caroline Helstone. What she has to say on these topics comes over as a lecture rather than the outpourings of a living soul. It is only as a woman, in love with Shirley's handsome and vigorous (though not entirely likeable) mill tenant, Robert Moore, that she touches our deeper sympathies.

In *Jane Eyre,* love swept everything aside once it entered the story. Jane's very ideas of feminine self-respect were in danger, because of it. In *Shirley* ideas reign supreme. We frequently find ourselves wondering how it is that feelings – which, here, are principally those of young women for eligible men – can be put on ice for such long periods, while social and moral issues are discussed, and rediscussed.

From the outset *Shirley* feels different from anything else Charlotte Brontë wrote. There is a more of a broad sense of Yorkshire society than in *Jane Eyre,* where human existence is a predominantly solitary or family affair. In spite of the era of social unrest in which it is set – the Luddite riots of 1811-12 – it is a kindlier novel than *Jane Eyre, Villette* or *The Professor.* (Even the weather seems to be un-characteristically clement, and the countryside appears to have lost its craggy and forbidding aspect.) The tone of the famous opening is genial in a manner quite un-Brontëan.

> Of late years an abundant shower of curates has fallen upon the North of England: they lie very thick upon the hills; every parish has one or more of them; they are young enough to be very active, and ought to be doing a great deal of good.

There follows a good deal of discussion of government decisions which, in restraining trade with Napoleonic Europe, have affected the manufacturing life of the North of England; of the need for modernisation of industrial plant; of the hardships this implies for those put out of work by these advances. But, try as she might, and research as she clearly did in the columns of the *Leeds Mercury* between 1812 and 1814, Charlotte Brontë cannot bring these issues alive on the page. Even the most heated debates lack urgency. The atmosphere is as close to humorous as one will ever find in a Charlotte Brontë novel. The bluntly spoken, radical Hiram Yorke is attacking the government:

> "What chance was there of being heard in a land that was king-ridden, peer-ridden, priest-ridden; where a lunatic was the nominal monarch, an unprincipled debauchee the real ruler; where such an insult to common sense as hereditary legislators was tolerated; where such a humbug as a bench of bishops, such an arrogant abuse as a pampered, persecuting established church was endured and venerated ..."

There *is* moral indignation here, but it is not the moral indignation which so effortlessly enlisted our sympathies in the attack on religious humbug in *Jane Eyre*. We chuckle at the felicity of the language rather than thrill in agreement with the strictures expressed.

It is when Charlotte Brontë leaves the broad canvas of contemporary social issues and embodies them in their effects on individual lives that she recovers her accustomed narrative power. Robert Moore, though not constitutionally a hard man, is as tenant of a cloth mill, in a race against time. With business badly hit by the war, he must bring in new weaving frames to maximise his profit on the reduced production available to him. This means laying off employees. He confronts a workers' deputation with a loaded pistol. Into the mouth of its spokesman, William Farren, Charlotte puts a speech which is eloquent of the sufferings of the millhands:

> 'It's out o' no ill-will that I'm here, for my part; it's just to mak a effort to get things straightened, for they're sorely a-crooked. Ye see we're all ill off – varry ill off; wer families is poor and pined. We're thrown out o' work with these frames; we can get nought we can earn nought. What is to be done? Mun we say, wisht! and to do us down and dee? Nay; I've no grand words at my tongue's end, Mr Moore, but I feel that it wad be a low

principle for a reasonable man to starve to death like a dumb
cratur .. "

The plea falls on deaf ears. Moore refuses to grant the men more time to adjust their domestic economies to the new circumstances. Although of an instinctively conservative disposition, politically speaking, and in general on the side of the mill-owners against the rioters, Charlotte Brontë has too much of the artist in her not to respond instinctively to the pathos of this situation.

> His [Moore's] last words had left a harsh impression; he at least had "failed in the disposing of a chance he was lord of." By speaking kindly to William Farren who was a very honest man, without envy or hatred of those more happily circum- stanced than himself, thinking it no hardship and no injustice to be forced to live by labour, disposed to be honourably content if he could but get work to do – Moore might have made a friend ... The poor fellow's face looked haggard with want; he had the aspect of a man who had not known what it was to live in comfort and plenty for weeks, perhaps months, past, and yet there was no ferocity, no malignity in his countenance ...

Charlotte Brontë then takes us home to Farren's hovel, where his wife is trying to stretch a dinner of porridge to feed his numerous offspring. Set back in time though this is, it powerfully evokes the feel of poverty as Charlotte Brontë would have witnessed it every day of her life. It is the stuff of which the 'big' social novel is made. But the promise held out by such scenes as this is never fulfilled. When we next see Moore defending his mill against assault, and later being wounded by a renegade agitator, it is as if Charlotte has forgotten the sympathy due to those workers who are the victims of industrial progress. She, too, seems to have failed in the disposing of a chance she was lord of. In the meantime, Caroline, in the throes of despised love for Robert, has gone into a somewhat theatrical physical decline. When she badgers her uncle, who is her ward, to let her get a job governessing, to give her some mental occupation, he pooh-poohs the suggestion and tells her to "run away and amuse yourself". "What with? My doll?" she ripostes.

Help, in the form of a new focus of interest for Caroline, is at hand with the entry of Shirley herself into the story. If the character of Shirley was intended to be a piece of homage to Emily (and the evidence is there in her love of large dogs, masculine pursuits, and a tendency to cauterise herself with hot irons when bitten by potentially rabid strays) then it is a piece of homage that has gone horribly wrong. Shirley is a sort of Emma of the Ridings; but unlike Jane Austen's Emma she is not subjected to that ironical scrutiny from her creator which makes the latter's faults palatable (and wholly enjoyable). She is just as patronising as Emma, but we are clearly not meant to think her so. She breezes into the room, articulate and self-assured. She soon decides to 'take up' Caroline, and within a very few pages there is a blaze of intimacy between these two wholly dissimilar spirits. One is conscious that it somewhat suits Charlotte Brontë that this should be so. Pages of girl talk between the pair furnish her with an opportunity to unload much thought about the state of relations between men and women in the early 19th century, as seen from the woman's standpoint. There is, of course, nothing at all wrong with this as a principle. But, wholesome and just though many of the pair's conclusions on the topic may be, we are conscious of being force-fed with them.

On their very first day out together ("Shirley easily persuaded Caroline to go with her ...") they are soon, without preamble, exchanging intimate reveries on their ideal landscape and the weather that would accompany it. The normally reticent Caroline opens these exchanges with her older companion, as if she had known her all her life. These are the first words she speaks to her in the novel. When previously asked for an opinion by Shirley (admittedly it had been for a character sketch of Robert Moore, a touchy subject) she had been unable to reply. But now:

"I know how the heath would look on such a day... purple black – a deeper shade of the sky tint, and that would be livid."
"Yes, quite livid, with brassy edges to the clouds, and here and there a white gleam, more ghastly than the lurid tinge, which, as you looked at it, you momentarily expected would kindle into blinding lightning."
"Did it thunder?"
"It muttered distant peals, but the storm did not break till evening, after we had reached our inn – that inn being an isolated house at the foot of a range of mountains."

There is something artificial about this whimsy from which rational judgement dissents. Had it gone on much longer in this vein, we would have expected the inn to be peopled with characters from Angria with Arthur Wellesley at their head. It is studiedly girlish in a way which runs quite contrary to the characters of either young woman as we see them illustrated elsewhere.

From landscape they move on to men. Charlotte Brontë seems to have forgotten that only a few pages before, Caroline was struck dumb at the mere thought of Robert Moore. Now, she introduces the topic herself, rhapsodising uninhibitedly on his "fine eyes", "well-cut features" and "dear, princely forehead", as if he was her accepted lover or fiancé.

And Shirley seems determined to surge ahead of her friend in her approbation of the subject.

"He is a noble being. I tell you when they are good, they are the lords of the creation – they are the sons of God ... Indisputably, a great, good, handsome man is the first of created things."
"Above us?"
"I would scorn to contend for empire with him – I would scorn it ..." "Men and women, husbands and wives, quarrel horribly, Shirley."
"Poor things! Poor fallen, degenerate things! God made them for another lot, for other feelings."
"But we are men's equals, or are we not?"

"Nothing ever charms me more than when I meet my superior
– one who makes me sincerely feel that he is my superior."
"Did you ever meet him?"
"I should be glad to see him any day. The higher above me so
much the better …"

The lofty philosophising of Shirley's twenty-one years seems here
less soundly based than the quiet scepticism of Caroline's eighteen.
There is an ecstatic quality about Shirley's rapture which so manifestly
parts company with good sense that we cannot help wondering what
the author's purpose is. Moore has his qualities, but he is certainly
not a "noble being", as Shirley is clearly aware when she rejects his
suit to her – and as we continuously see from his offhand treatment of
Caroline and of his own mill hands. Charlotte Brontë seems, yet again,
to be succumbing to that compulsion to worship which was an ever-
present component of her psyche where the business of loving men
was concerned. To desire to be in harness with a character whose
qualities she could merely unreservedly admire never seemed to be
enough. She must adore, with all the pain that such a loss of perspective
might, and in her case did, entail.

Shirley's outburst is the less convincing for the fact that she is the
least likely woman in all the pages of Charlotte Brontë fiction to have
uttered it. But, as Susan Gubar recognises,

Shirley seems slightly unreal to most readers and this very
unreality serves to remind us that she is part of a fantastic wish
fulfilment, an affirmation of what ought to be possible for
women.

The entry of Shirley nevertheless holds out the promise of a
quickened tempo in the novel. Yet, with all her personal endowments
and social position, Charlotte never creates for her a focal role. (At
one point she removes Shirley from the scene of the action for fifty
odd pages, without our really missing her.) Events come crowding
in. But their promiscuous diversity has the reader continuously groping
for the novel's moral core. Moore is attacked in his mill by disaffected

workers; Caroline learns that Shirley's governess, Mrs Pryor, is her mother; Shirley refuses numerous offers of marriage; Moore is seriously wounded in an assassination attempt on him.

But in the end, in spite of the ambitious social canvas on which *Shirley* is sketched out, it is the wildly beating heart of Caroline Helstone which is at the centre of the book. Charlotte Brontë cannot thread its other elements: war; industrial strife; social conscience; the plight of women; onto her fictional string and make them organic to her purposes. Moments of social history are explored with the intensity and honesty we would expect of a writer of Charlotte's skill – and then forgotten. We hear of ignorant armies clashing by night, but she cannot make us *care* about them.

At the dénouement, it is personal destinies, not social issues, that have been resolved. In a final 'tidying up', the heroines 'get' their men. Caroline marries a now 'kinder' Robert Moore, who has lately acquired a conscience and promises to use the profits of any industrial success he may have, to do social good. Shirley takes Robert's shadowy brother Louis, who, with her encouragement, will become the area's wise magistrate, a man in harmony with his brother's benevolent plans. The bells ringing throughout England to celebrate Wellington's victory at Salamanca are made to echo the wedding chimes of the two couples. But they only serve uncomfortably to remind us that in *Shirley* history is never, in fact, successfully appropriated for the purposes of fiction.

8 VILLETTE, THE PROFESSOR

VILLETTE has been the most vehemently argued over of all Charlotte Brontë's novels. For many, it has an integrity of purpose not to be found in Jane Eyre and is the book which represents the true flowering of her genius. George Eliot, writing contemporaneously with its publication, felt that there was "something almost preternatural in its power". For G. H. Lewes it was "an influence of truth as healthful as a mountain breeze". Matthew Arnold, however, found it "Hideous, undelightful, convulsed, constricted ... one of the most utterly disagreeable books I have ever read". But it is Thackeray, in a wry aside, who perhaps describes the difficulties we have with the novel better than any of the foregoing: "That's a plaguey book that Villette. How clever it is – and how I don't like the heroine."

Whether or not Villette is a faithful description of Charlotte's relations with the Pensionnat Heger and its proprietor (and clearly it owes much to both) need not detain us from a critical point of view. In translating experience on to paper writers do not – could not, even if they would – simply copy life. Besides, there are many other sources, ones quite outside the Brussels experience, for the character portraits in Villette.

So exclusively is the action of the novel seen and analysed through the perceptions of its protagonist, Lucy Snowe, that much depends on the reader's view of her. And the fact is that Villette, as narrated by Lucy, is an ineluctably dreary book. Its heroine, misanthropic, neurasthenic and not a little pharisaical, gives short shrift to the brighter, much less the lighter, side of human nature. For much of the book she is little more than a spectator – and a bitterly critical one at that – at life's feast. Not one character in the story – not even her admired M Paul whose Roman Catholicism is a blemish she must continually try to argue away – escapes her acid scrutiny.

The very setting of the book, and Charlotte's handling of it, are equivocal. Why has metropolitan Brussels become Villette, a mere townlet? Why must it be reached through an embarkation port named

Boue- (mud, sludge) *Marine?* And why is the whole located in a country unflatteringly styled *Labassecour* (the farmyard)? Is Charlotte simply having a little fun with us? Are these things merely the excrescences of a mind too exclusively bent on higher things to be bothered with thinking up more appropriate place names? Or do they indicate a subconscious loathing of an experience she could never look back on without rage and shame?

Her portrait of Brussels and Belgian life has often been commented on as a masterly evocation. But is this what we get in *Villette?* Where is the teeming humanity of the Belgian capital? When does Lucy ever venture out into the cosmopolitan life of its street cafés? Where do we ever feel its spacious squares, promenades and fountains? Instead, Lucy's Villette is a narrow, constricting and gloomy city, all shadows, allées défendues, churches and graveyards. We are scarcely surprised that she suffers a mental breakdown in such a place.

As for the Belgians – and their Roman Catholicism – they are treated by Lucy/Charlotte with a prejudice that borders on the pathological. On one occasion, her mind totally unhinged after weeks of solitude, Lucy enters a church and seeks the consolation of the confessional. Her confessor, a thoughtful and compassionate man, hears her out in a manner which soothes her troubled spirit. Realising that the formulaic jargon of the absolution is not appropriate to her condition or her Protestant faith, he offers her personal spiritual counselling at his house on the following day. But the mere fact of having poured out her troubles has already solaced her. Her stout Protestant heart will not falter again.

> Did I, do you suppose, reader, contemplate venturing again within that worthy priest's reach? As soon should I have thought of walking into a Babylonish furnace.

This seems a churlish recompense for her confessor's total honesty with her. She is later to meet her saviour, Père Silas, again. On this occasion she inflicts on the reader an even more vehement rejection of all Catholicism's tenets and rituals. We feel a certain sympathy with that part of Harriet Martineau's hostile review of *Villette* in the *Daily News* of 3rd February 1853 which remonstrated mildly:

We do not exactly see the moral necessity for this (there is no artistical necessity) and we are rather sorry for it, occurring as it does at a time when catholics and protestants hate each other quite sufficiently ...

Villette opens with a handful of chapters set in England which are in such marked contrast in mood to what follows them that they scarcely seem to inhabit the same novel. The orphaned Lucy is on an extended visit at the house of her godmother Mrs Bretton. Into this menage is suddenly introduced Paulina, a six-year-old relation, whose mother has died. The grief-stricken but nevertheless resolute and winsome child strikes up an adoring relationship with Graham, the sixteen-year-old son of the family. The atmosphere is, if not exactly sunny, then at least kindly. Mrs Bretton is a benevolent spirit. Graham is an attractive young man whose gently, though occasionally thoughtlessly, exercised power over his tiny admirer seems to promise that he will be a favourite with women in the future. The passages between him and the little girl are charmingly done, and quite escape the mawkishness to which such scenes are, in general, only too prone.

But when, ten years later, we meet the pair again in Villette the world has become an older and sourer place. Graham Bretton is now seen as a flawed, limited figure. The determined, eccentric little body of six has grown up into a pretty, but lifeless, doll of seventeen. Their creator permits them to marry. But we are left under no illusion that it is a union of inferior spirits. Had Bretton been a better man he would have chosen Lucy. Though she assents to his marriage, she cannot really forgive him.

For Lucy, Villette and the continental wiles for which it stands, are in marked contrast to the innocence of the old England she has left. And though she chooses to make her life in Labassecour, she never appears to be at home there. Appointed a teacher at the pensionnat of Madame Beck, from the outset she has no patience with her

Labassecourienne charges.

> Imprimis – it was as clear as the day that this swinish multitude
> were not to be driven by force. They were to be humoured,
> borne with very patiently: a courteous though sedate manner
> impressed them; a flash of raillery did good. Severe or
> continuous mental application they could not, or would not,
> bear: heavy demand on the memory, the reason, the attention,
> they rejected point-blank. Where an English girl of not more
> than average capacity and docility, would quietly take a theme
> and bind herself to the task of comprehension and mastery, a
> Labassecourienne would laugh in your face, and throw it back
> to you with the phrase, – "Dieu que c'est difficile! Je n'en veux
> pas. Cela m'ennuie trop."

The natives of the farmyard cannot hold a candle to their stalwart
English counterparts. And they have the cheek to protest their
inadequacies in French. It is sad to see such rank chauvinism distorting
the perceptions of a spirit as honest as Charlotte Brontë's normally
is. Since it is inconceivable that among all those pupils she
encountered, not one exhibited the glimmerings of intelligence and
an ability to learn, we can only assume that an excoriating memory
has forced its way to the surface, here: to the trials of pupil stupidity
are added the fact that the Protestant English teacher has found herself
in a Catholic country.

But a more specific source of affliction awaits her. One of her pupils,
Ginevra Fanshawe, who had, to her credit, befriended her on the packet
boat, is sporting with the affections of a man Lucy is, too, disposed to
admire, the Pensionnat's medical attendant, Dr John. (He is later to
be revealed to us as the Graham Bretton of ten years before.)

Ginevra is a harmless enough flirt. A Jane Austen or a Thackeray
would have let her off with an ironical smack on the bottom. To Lucy,
Ginevra is another Adèle, but an Adèle who has already eaten the
Apple. Her determination to flirt with two men at once (she also has
a second admirer, an army officer) is a moral offence. Ginevra ought
to marry her first suitor. The girl disclaims any such intention in

unobjectionable enough terms:

> " ... the man is too romantic and devoted, and he expects more
> of me than I find it convenient to be. He thinks I am perfect:
> furnished with all sorts of sterling qualities and solid virtues,
> such as I never had, nor intend to have."

It takes a cumbersome authorial device, all too reminiscent of Rochester's, vis-à-vis Blanche, to remove the scales from Dr Bretton's eyes. In the meantime, having first-hand evidence of the degree, as well as of the earnest terms, of Dr John's self delusion, we are not inclined to dissent from Ginevra's assessment of his style of wooing. And in declining to admire *his* sterling qualities, she at least understands herself.

True, Ginevra can be thoughtless where Lucy's feelings are concerned. To her Lucy is a "nobody's daughter' and "twenty-three" – impossibly old from her standpoint. But having written the girl off as being completely illiterate and ineducable, Lucy (or Charlotte?) seems to have failed to notice that Ginevra's commonly-used nicknames for her, "Timon" and "Old Diogenes", and for Dr Bretton, "Esculapius", do, in fact, suggest an easy acquaintanceship with the classics, as well as being highly appropriate.

If there is no depth to her character she has, at least, an affectionate heart. She is one of the few characters of genuine vitality in a novel which desperately lacks high spirits. She has certainly never done Lucy any harm. Indeed it was she, on the cross-channel passage, who proposed the Pensionnat Beck as a solution to Lucy's indecision in the first place. And there is something ungenerous in the manner of Lucy's dismissal of her after her mésalliance with her foppish cavalier has actually come to pass.

Like Lydia Bennet she is hustled from the scene. Her Wickham, Colonel Alfred de Hamal, is, like his Jane Austen counterpart, constitutionally debt-ridden. In a strong echo of Lydia's plight, Ginevra in this uncomfortable marriage:

called out lustily for sympathy and aid. She had no notion of meeting any distress singlehanded. In some shape, from some quarter or other, she was pretty sure to obtain her will, and so she got on – fighting the battle of life by proxy ...

Thackeray, always astute on Charlotte Brontë, observed lightheartedly:

> *Villette* is rather vulgar – I don't make my good women ready to fall in love with two men at once, and Miss Brontë would be very angry with me and very fierce if I did.

To be fair to Miss Brontë, she makes M Paul Emanuel begin to fall in love with Lucy some time before the latter is aware of it. She is by that time weaning herself off Dr Bretton. Emanuel, to this point very much a background character, now steps towards the front of the book and dominates Lucy's consciousness during its last third. Charlotte Brontë clearly wants us to agree with her that his intellectuality, idealism, warmth and generosity make him the perfect mate for an independent spirit like Lucy's. The alliance of his academic standing and her desire to make a way in the teaching world, will be an ideal one.

But for all her strenuous efforts Emanuel will not stand up as a hero. He makes himself too ridiculous in public with his outbursts and petty jealousies. He is a ludicrous rather than comic figure. We laugh at him, not with him. As Leslie Stephen has remarked, his tempests of wrath breaking on the small canvas of an insignificant pensionnat make him merely "an Aeolus of the duck-pond". He never gets the opportunity to develop the great qualities we are asked to believe in, in a larger sphere. For Charlotte's sake, we would prefer to think that this merely fiery little pedagogue is not actually the man to whom she once abased herself in such nakedness of soul.

The ending of *Villette* is left ambiguous. M Paul is removed through some cumbersome mechanics of plot to Guadeloupe for three years. Back in Villette, Lucy tends and expands the academy they have founded. We are not certain whether or not his ship survives an Atlantic storm to reunite him with Lucy. It is not meant to matter. In Lucy's mind they have already won through to love, even if, at the end, her Protestant soul must still be worrying over the gulf between their respective religious ideologies.

> All Rome could not put him into bigotry, nor the Propaganda itself make him a real Jesuit. He was born honest, and not false – artless and not cunning – a freeman and not a slave. His tenderness had rendered him ductile in a priest's hands, his affection, his devotedness, his sincere pious enthusiasm blinded his kind eyes sometimes, made him abandon justice to himself to do the work of craft and serve the ends of selfishness ...

This is surely the most hedged-about tribute to a beloved object to be encountered anywhere in fiction.

Lewes qualified his enthusiasm for *Villette* by noting that it was not a novel in the normal sense of the word:

> Much of the book seems to be brought in merely that the writer may express something which is in her mind.

This is astute. The chief fault of *Villette* is that analysis predominates over creative imagination, and ends up throttling it. Thus, when Charlotte wants Lucy to recover from her love for Dr Bretton she does so not by showing us his character in action but by supplying her with the following highly-tendentious assessment.

> Dr John *could* think ... but he was rather a man of action than of thought; he *could* feel, and feel vividly in his own way, but his heart had no chord for enthusiasm: to bright, soft, sweet influences his eyes and lips gave bright, soft, sweet welcome... for what belonged to storm, what was wild and intense, dangerous, sudden and flaming, he had no sympathy, and held with it no communion.

This is rough handling of a man whose only crime is that he has not been able to reciprocate her love for him. Yet it is treatment which proceeds naturally enough from the unforgiving mind that functions in the moral engine room of this argumentative, yet emotionally incoherent, novel. The weight of Lucy's expectation lies so heavy on whatever, or whoever, she attaches herself to, that we tremble for the result. Where her desires are unassuaged she strikes out ruthlessly at those who disappoint her. In all her creative *oeuvre,* Charlotte Brontë was never more disillusioned, never less in love with life, than she was in *Villette.*

The Professor, published posthumously in 1857, does not add anything to Charlotte Brontë's reputation. But it is worth reading, and Smith, Elder were astute to see that its author was capable of fiction of arresting quality.

In a sense, it is a sketch for *Villette,* though one with significant differences. Its young protagonist, William Crimsworth, tiring of the servitude of working for his exacting and brutal brother at his Yorkshire mill, decides to make a life for himself in Brussels. There he obtains teaching posts at both a boys' and a girls' school. The latter is run by the coquettish Mlle Reuter, who, notwithstanding that she is about to be married to M Pelet, the headmaster of the boys' school, is disposed to like Crimsworth. He evades her intentions, and, having fallen in love with one of his pupils, eventually marries her and takes her back to Yorkshire.

Having a man as protagonist has its advantages for Charlotte. It gives her the authorial opportunity to put herself inside 'male' situations in a way denied to her in the other novels. Thus, when Pelet and Mlle Reuter are about to tie the knot, he decides he must leave Pelet's house where he has been lodging, since

> ... if I stayed the probability was that in three months' time a
> practical modern French novel would be in full process of
> concoction under the roof of the unsuspecting Pelet.

Interestingly, Charlotte can allow to a male protagonist a moral freedom – even if it is merely one of thought – she would never dream of according to Jane Eyre, Caroline Helstone or Lucy Snowe. A Dickens hero would never have been allowed thus to soliloquise. Small wonder that Mrs Gaskell, when considering the novel's publication, cried out in anguish to George Smith

> But oh! I wish Mr Nicholls wd have altered more! ... For I
> would not, if I could help it, have another syllable that could
> be called coarse to be associated with her name ...

There is little else in the novel to surprise. Tellingly, the preliminary scenes of family conflict in Yorkshire are set in a much fiercer, more bracing, moral climate than we ever experience after the transfer to Brussels. Crimsworth has all Charlotte's anti-Popish prejudices and he finds teaching Belgians as little stimulating as she/Lucy Snowe do.

Indeed, these aspects of both *The Professor* and *Villette* prompt a question which seems to me fundamental. However powerful it was in some respects, was Charlotte's Brussels experience not, in fact, a creative disaster for her? To a novelist, Brussels and the Pensionnat Heger were doubtless good for some exotic detail, and for the chance to conduct extended passages of dialogue in French (though the non-French speaker may justly find these irritating). As background they impart to *Villette* and *The Professor* a patina of sophistication. But it is the Yorkshire novel *Jane Eyre* which is her masterpiece. Nothing she did afterwards was to approach it.

9 EMILY BRONTË: *WUTHERING HEIGHTS*

WUTHERING HEIGHTS has long since risen above the chorus of condemnation that greeted its publication – a reaction of such revulsion that, as we have seen, Charlotte felt it necessary to excuse her sister's naïveté and lack of experience in the preface she wrote to the 1850 edition of the novel. She went so far as to say:

> Whether it is right or advisable to create beings like Heathcliff
> I do not know: I scarcely think it is. But this I know: the writer
> who possesses the creative gift owns something of which he is
> not always master.

thus establishing Emily as a wild creature who scarcely knew what she wrote. The notion has not been an easy one to dispel. If the chorus of disapproval has died down, subsequent critical reaction to the novel has been of the sort that does not make it any easier to say why – or even if – *Wuthering Heights* is a great book. In his *The Great Tradition*, F. R. Leavis allowed it to be an "astonishing work". But he excepted it from his consideration, as "a kind of sport", as if its qualities implied some unacceptable deviation from the healthy novelistic norm, which was in its turn likely to spawn even more misthwart offspring. (Among these he included George Douglas's *The House with the Green Shutters*, an undoubtedly powerful work but one having no kinship with *Wuthering Heights*.)

A more deadly form of approval has been that which sees *Wuthering Heights* as the natural offspring of Shakespearean tragedy. Thus, parallels are drawn with *King Lear* – though for no other perceivable reason than that blasted heaths feature in both. *Macbeth*, too, has been drafted in as an antecedent, while Heathcliff has been deprecated (or praised) as "the greatest villain since Iago".

The battle for the novel's heart ranges, too, over the question of whether we can – or even should – think of *Wuthering Heights* as realistic. Is it "a nightmare of the superheated imagination", poetical, mystical, fabulous? Or is it, like *The Archers,* a recognisable "tale of country folk"? Is its scenery, even, that of the West Riding which Emily knew so well, or are her landscapes, rather, culled and recreated from the Scottish borderlands of the Scott novels she read so copiously?

As for the novel's structure, is it a patched, crude and implausible piece of storytelling, redeemed only by the power of the tale itself? Or is it a carefully forged piece of narrative whose shifts of perspective are germane to the whole?

The question of the realism of *Wuthering Heights* is the most easily dispensed with. All the Brontë novels are strong on physical atmosphere. But Emily has no peer among her sisters for the weight of detail she assembles to convey an irresistible conviction of events sharply experienced. From the very outset Wuthering Heights *lives,* as a building, as perhaps no other house in fiction. It stands before us not as a figment of the Gothic imagination but as a hard-favoured working farmhouse.

From the moment Lockwood's horse breasts the farmyard gate and he crosses the threshold we are intensely aware of Heathcliff's dwelling place, from the large jagged stones which comprise its exterior structure to the array of pewter dishes, silver jugs, tankards, shotguns and horse pistols which strew its gloomy interior. Yet there was never a less stagey piece of scene setting than this. We, like the uninvited Lockwood, only gradually penetrate the house, in the teeth of the palpable reluctance of its denizens to let us in. Like him, we assimilate domestic detail in snatches, on the way. The very dogs which haunt its recesses and passages are the creation of one who knows farm canines and their behaviour to strangers. When Lockwood imprudently tries to fondle a pointer bitch and is full-throatedly attacked by her and her brood for his pains, Heathcliff's unconcerned reaction to the event is the entirely authentic response of the countryman.

> "They won't meddle with persons who touch nothing," he
> remarked, putting the bottle of wine before me, and restoring

the displaced table. "The dogs do right to be vigilant. Take a glass of wine?"

Whoever she is employing as narrator, Emily Brontë effortlessly sustains her fidelity of observation. Later in the book (though earlier, now, in time) Hindley Earnshaw threatens the young foundling Heathcliff "with an iron weight used for weighing potatoes and hay". Only someone intimately acquainted with farm usage could possibly have thought up such an instrument of chastisement. A lesser writer would have employed some more obviously throwable agricultural implement: pitchfork, spade or rake. But Emily knows that the ½ cwt lump of iron with its convenient handle, inset for ease of lifting, makes an ideal close-quarters missile for someone really strong. And so it proves as Hindley hurls it at Heathcliff, hitting him on the chest and knocking him flat.

Wherever violence occurs, Emily describes it and its effects with dispassionate correctness. She has no need to seek refuge in that generalised fictional vocabulary which uses livid weals and purple bruises as its epithets. When the younger Catherine is hit around the head by Heathcliff, she insists on enlisting her cowardly cousin, Linton Heathcliff, who is shortly to become her husband, as a witness to the extent of her injuries. He later describes them to Nelly:

> her cheek, cut on the inside, against her teeth, and her mouth filling with blood... she has never spoken to me since: and I sometimes think she can't speak for pain ...

This is observed by someone who knows at first hand what a good crack over the face feels like, and, though it may leave no exterior bruising to betray the perpetrator, what sort of internal damage it can inflict.

At the opposite pole of experience, though requiring the same degree of observation, is Emily Brontë's exquisite sensitivity to the atmosphere of her native uplands. As Cathy recuperates from a fever which has had her in thrall throughout much of the winter, the yellow crocuses her husband lays beside her on her pillow, speak to her urgently of the spring she is still too ill go outdoors to see. She asks him:

> "Edgar, is there not a south wind, and is not the snow almost gone?"
> "The snow is quite gone down here, darling," replied her husband; and I can only see two white spots on the whole range of moors; the sky is blue, and the larks are singing, and the becks and brooks are all brim full ..."

The description is one of unvarnished simplicity. But it is eloquent of that sensation the northerner feels when winter suddenly loosens its grip, springs flow again, and nature quickens.

One more example will serve to prove the point. Catherine II is riding out with Ellen to make a promised rendezvous with Linton Heathcliff on the moors. It is some time towards the end of summer.

> It was a close sultry day: devoid of sunshine, but with a sky too dappled and hazy to threaten rain.

No other author would have bothered with these details. They have nothing specific to do with the dynamics of the plot at this point. But Emily Brontë was too steeped in the influence of wind and weather to let a ride on the moors go ahead without including them. And what she has to say about the cloud cover is totally authentic. What she describes is high-riding altocumulus – in the vernacular, mackerel sky. As she correctly asserts, the sun will not break through today, but there is no fear of rain. Incidentally, such an atmosphere will not prove good for the peevish and weak-chested Linton.

Until Hardy, no other English novelist was to describe climate, the *feel* of weather as it affects human beings, with such unforced accuracy.

The problem of structure in *Wuthering Heights* is one in which it is all too easy to become bogged down. It is perhaps only fair to admit that even if for a moment we agreed that the narrative was clumsy – and some still find it so – then the power of the material would probably survive that defect. But in fact, the method – the use of two principal narrators but, importantly, a number of 'subsidiaries'– is, far from being merely a device to get the plot to work. It provides us with vital and subtle shifts of viewpoint, as well as a freedom of moral movement which both Charlotte and Anne are denied as novelists. Charlotte pours out her naked prejudices on paper through the mouths of protagonists who are recognisably herself. If far less dogmatic, Anne makes clear that her characters are bound by moral laws she herself respects. But Emily is never betrayed into editorialising. There is not one opinion uttered by any character in *Wuthering Heights* that we could safely say is hers.

Lockwood is not merely a mechanical device to set the action going. He is an essential part of the reader's standpoint. Without him, we would not perceive Heathcliff's house and its denizens in action, in the way we do. He is the *homme moyen* of the drawing room in all of us. His reaction to his reception at Wuthering Heights is the shocked, but at the same time slightly condescending, response of urban (and here southern) assumptions when they are exposed to the rough manners of rural society.

When Ellen, the countrywoman, takes up the running as narrator, the viewpoint on the action shifts. But it does so seamlessly, and we are scarcely aware of the transition to matter-of-fact acceptance of a culture Lockwood found so unfamiliar and alarming. Besides being narrator, Nelly is go-between, spy, and bucolic moralist. Other minor narrators: Isabella, Linton, Zillah, are used to fill in points in the action on which she could not be expected to have full knowledge. These interjections, too, are handled with consummate artistry. They not only further illuminate the character of each narrator for us, they shed fresh light on the characters commented on. And we are not even aware of the device.

As for the plot of this supposedly wild effusion, it can be seen as a thing of almost geometrical symmetry. (It is actually far easier – and quicker – to represent diagrammatically than to describe in words).

The two houses, Wuthering Heights (Earnshaw) and Thrushcross

Grange (Linton), represent, respectively, the wild, uncouth life of the high moors and an effete, or at least over-refined, society of the lower valleys. Catherine (Earnshaw) marries Edgar (Linton), the son of the Grange. In doing so, she 'goes over to the other side,' temporarily betraying the rugged culture of Wuthering Heights (and Heathcliff, its even more rugged adopted son, who loves, and is loved by, her). But in giving birth to a daughter (also Catherine) she dies. When she comes of age, this Catherine (Linton) is tricked into marrying her cousin, Linton (Heathcliff), the son of the man her mother had loved. By this time Heathcliff senior has supplanted the Earnshaws at Wuthering Heights. Shortly afterwards, Catherine's own father dies. Since his estate had been entailed on his sister, whom Heathcliff has married, Thrushcross Grange, too, falls into Heathcliff's hands. The pampered Thrushcross-bred Catherine is forced to go and live at Wuthering Heights. She now seems irrevocably a Heathcliff herself. But her young husband dies. His father, Heathcliff, eventually follows him. Catherine is now able to marry her other cousin Hareton Earnshaw, whose rights to Wuthering Heights had been usurped by Heathcliff in the first place. In this resolution, Heathcliff, the catalyst of the entire action, is physically eliminated, leaving those whose lives he had always wanted to blight, to inherit the earth. Catherine returns to the Earnshaw spiritual fold, which her mother had deserted.

As this attempt to summarise the plot indicates, its architecture is far too complex, its components far too interdependent, not to have been deeply meditated. The wonder is that in the reading of it, the mechanics by which it functions are so utterly subsumed in the overriding passions they serve, that we do not notice them.

Which returns us to the first and most fundamental question: what sort of book is *Wuthering Heights?* What does it mean? Are the protagonists a pair of marvellous beings? Or is Heathcliff simply evil, and Cathy's love for him in the full knowledge of that, a grotesque distortion of human nature? Is their love, even if genuine, nevertheless a morbid one? Has passion gone mad? become purely destructive? And if the story is tragic, as Swinburne and others have insisted, whose tragedy is it?

In his otherwise generally helpful essay *The Originality of Wuthering Heights* Keith Sagar attempts the following approach to the book.

> I believe that *Wuthering Heights* demands to be read in such a way that Heathcliff functions simultaneously on three levels, none of which, alone, can account for him. On the surface he functions as an autonomous character in a drama whose meanings are ethical and social; first exemplifying the evil effects of cruelty, deprivation and conventional education on the young; then as a critic of the artificial social and moral refinement of the Lintons; finally as a man destroyed by sterile passions of hate and revenge.

This is a worthy and responsible sort of criticism. But it so manifestly fails to engage with the inescapably *exhilarating* atmosphere of *Wuthering Heights* that we instinctively shake our heads at it. As V. S. Pritchett has acutely remarked, there is in the novel a complete lack of psychological dismay. Hating is done with zest. Blows are traded with a wolfish smile on the face. The recipients of punishment, even if they are young women, are implacably sworn to revenge. There is about it all a magnificent vitality which sweeps aside considerations of right and wrong. When Heathcliff strikes the young Catherine Linton and cuts her face, we feel none of the moral indignation we did at the psychological cruelty inflicted on Jane Eyre by Aunt Reed or Brocklehurst. Rather we are intrigued by the manner in which Catherine steels herself mentally to be strong against the next assault. She is obdurate under chastisement. And our curiosity, and our admiration of her far outweigh any disapproval we might feel of Heathcliff.

In this atmosphere, the love of Cathy and Heathcliff is sustained by each at a pitch of self absorption which not only cares nothing for the sufferings it inflicts on others, but is careless of *anything* outside its immediate self. In his last meeting with the fatally ill Catherine, Heathcliff, who has gained admission to Thrushcross Grange in the temporary absence of Edgar, crushes her to him in a passion of despair and thwarted love. But although she stands on the threshold of eternity she can still heap reproaches on him.

> "You and Edgar have both broken my heart, Heathcliff! And you both came to bewail the deed to me as if *you* were the people to be pitied! I shall not pity you, not I. You have killed me – and thriven on it, I think. How strong you are! How many years do you mean to live after I am gone?"

This is not mere petulance. The ego is too tremendous for that. It is of a piece with everything in this pair's loving. Its sheer magnitude redeems it. It is a love which refuses to brook separation in this life, and does not want to accept it after death.

Earlier Cathy had said to her husband, as he cradled her in his arms:

> " ... you'll leave me and I shall remain for ever. Next spring you'll long again to have me under this roof, and you'll look back and think you were happy today ..."

The selfishness is breathtaking. Yet it embraces Edgar and confers a kind of immortality on him, too. Cathy is right. He has been privileged to love. He knows that, and will carry her memory to his own grave.

There is ringing pathos in this. Yet neither it, nor the love of Heathcliff and Cathy are the stuff of tragedy. There is nothing star-crossed or fate-thwarted about the pair. The effects of their love do not leave us thinking of what might have been, had things gone differently. They have created their own plane of existence – one of violent ecstasy – and they will obstinately inhabit it. A mad, or at least foolishly-argued, impulse made Cathy think that marrying Edgar was the right thing to do. Knowing she was still in love with Heathcliff, she was quite prepared to commit spiritual bigamy. It does not matter. Heathcliff will, in his own way, 'get her' in the end.

When he does, it is as a man emptied of hatred. Yet this is not the tragic purging of a Lear when he confronts Cordelia for the last time. The gale of tremendous anger which has so dominated the book has simply blown itself out. Heathcliff might still accomplish his purposes of vengeance. But he no longer knows what they are. He has looked into the faces of Hareton and Catherine II and seen an echo of his great love there. He knows – to appropriate Yeats – that this is no country for old men. The young are already in one another's arms. They must be allowed to get on with it. He did not foresee this end to it all, but is redeemed, at the last, by his acceptance of it. And then, having run out of steam – he dies.

His death is, of course, clinically implausible. No one in the book was less likely to fade away in this manner than Heathcliff. But he must be got offstage, now. It is one of the two pieces of theatrical business Emily permits herself in the book. The other was earlier, where Heathcliff managed to get himself out of earshot so rapidly that, having heard with rapt and painful attention the first part of Cathy's declaration: "It would degrade me to marry Heathcliff now;" he completely misses the second half of her sentence: "so he shall never know how much I love him."

We forgive both pieces of business. Neither give rise to psychological untruth. Cathy could never have married Heathcliff, and it is impossible to imagine a Nahum Tate-style rewrite of the scenario which would not render the idea absurd. As for Heathcliff's death, like that of Enobarbus (equally defying pathological analysis), it has, by that time become inevitable.

Indeed, Shakespeare's Antony and Cleopatra and Heathcliff and Cathy have something fundamental in common, different though the atmosphere of the Roman and Mediterranean play is from that of the Northern and nineteenth century novel. Both assert the primacy of passion over anything else, and make it their ethic. We do not want Antony to achieve – or even share in – empire, any more than we can imagine Heathcliff and bourgeois domestic felicity reigning at Wuthering Heights. Both sets of protagonists are reckless of responsibility, giving us in its place a stupendous *egoisme à deux*. Neither are, in the end, the stuff of tragedy. Yet both offer us what R. H. Case, in his introduction to the play, has called: "a thrill, a quickening of the pulses, a brief experience in a region where there is an unimagined vividness of life".

10 ANNE BRONTË: *AGNES GREY,*
THE TENANT OF WILDFELL HALL

THE work of Anne Brontë is so often spoken of as meriting only a
footnote to the Haworth Parsonage *oeuvre* that her qualities as a
novelist are in danger of going completely unrecognised. She suffers
more than either of her sisters from the habit of reading from what we
(think we) know of her life and temperament into her novels. On the
literal level, this procedure will translate the curate who falls in love
with the heroine of *Agnes Grey* into William Weightman, Anne's
supposed love. Again, what we know – or think we know – of her
religious upbringing is made to colour whatever philosophical debate
takes place in her pages, especially that between women. But more
pernicious than either of these is the resolute tendency to see
'sweetness' in Anne, and from this to ascribe a placid, unconcerned,
even self-assured quality to her female protagonists.

The words 'sweet' and 'sincere' were first uttered in connection
with Anne's work by her sister Charlotte in her *Biographical Notice
of Ellis and Acton Bell,* published after their deaths, in 1850. They
have plagued her ever since. The implication of so much of the
criticism of her work is that such sweetness and sincerity are not the
tools with which moral truth is to be prised from the hard soil and
harder souls of the Yorkshire moors; that Anne did not have Charlotte's
or Emily's refining fire; that her docile nature somehow protected
her from the terrific conflicts which raged in them; that, as the
Edwardian scholar Sir Walter Raleigh said of Robert Bridges, there
was "a shade too little of the blackguard" in her to permit her to dive
down into the murky bottom of human nature and confront what she
might find there. It is surprising that such attitudes can have survived
the most cursory reading of her novels.

Certainly Anne is in many ways *different* as a writer, and as a
sensibility, from her sisters. But she had much more of Emily's steel
in her than has been allowed. She is completely free of Charlotte's
morbid sentiment. Neither of her women protagonists display the

faintest traces of masochism. Helen Huntingdon is a truly magnificent creation, a woman who stands up articulately to her brutal and womanising husband while courageously fending off those of his friends who try to exploit her vulnerability for their own sexual purposes.

Finally, in her unremitting, evocation of human cruelty to animals and fellow human beings alike, Anne Brontë draws on a wealth of experience with which she was utterly familiar. She does not have to strive after even her most chilling effects.

Agnes Grey falls some way short of being the perfectly achieved short novel it so clearly might have been. Its author's inexperience as a technician betray it. There are *longueurs* in the plotting. The curate, Weston, who loves Agnes, is not vividly enough realised to rivet us as he needs to. Yet in the stark realism of its setting, *Agnes Grey* stands comparison with anything of her sisters. None of them ever portrayed the sheer nastiness of pampered children with greater conviction.

Tom, the son of the Bloomfield family to whom Agnes has gone as governess, has found a birds' nest whose occupants he is looking forward to torturing to death.

> Mary Ann and Fanny, whom I was just bringing out, ran to admire his spoils, and to beg each a bird for themselves. "No, not one!" cried Tom. "They're all mine: Uncle Robson gave them to me – one, two, three, four, five – you shan't touch one of them! no, not one, for your lives!" continued he exultingly; laying the nest on the ground, and standing over it with his legs wide apart, his hands thrust into his breeches-pockets, his body bent forward, and his face twisted into all manner of contortions in the ecstasy of his delight.
>
> "But you shall see me fettle 'em off. My word, but I *will* wallop 'em! See if I don't now. By gum! but there's rare sport for me in that nest."

Agnes responds with a resolution the more admirable in that, far from having any parental support for her actions, she acts not only against the mother's disposition to indulge her son but against his father's active encouragement of cruelty.

> ... at the risk of both making myself sick and incurring the wrath of my employers – I got a large stone, that had been reared up for a mousetrap by the gardener, then, having once more vainly endeavoured to persuade the little tyrant to let the birds be carried back, I asked what he intended to do with them. With fiendish glee he commenced a list of torments; and while he was busied in the relation, I dropped the stone upon his intended victims and crushed them flat beneath it.

Yet, although Anne is so clearly familiar with this untroubled cruelty to animals, she does not let it blind her to the positive qualities to be found in the young, even in an overindulged family. In Matilda Murray, the younger daughter of the next family to which Agnes goes as governess, she has actually created a rather likeable tomboy. The elder Miss Murray has trapped her governess, intending to inflict on her an account of a ball they attended during the vacation.

> "No, – damn it, no!" shouted Miss Matilda. "Hold your tongue, can't ye? and let me tell her about my new mare – *such* a splendour, Miss Grey! a fine blood mare –"

And so Matilda continues through the book, swearing like a trooper, but harming nothing and no one.

Although *Agnes Grey* springs directly from the – clearly often highly unpleasant – experiences of Anne's governessing, it is not a shocked or bruised book. There is a freedom of sentiment, an unforced spontaneity of language in the exchanges between its characters which imparts a certain zest to its proceedings. And, notwithstanding her tribulations, its protagonist is free from self-pity. Agnes Grey is actually a much tougher character than either Caroline Helstone or Lucy Snowe.

The Tenant of Wildfell Hall is the most underrated of all the Brontë novels. Like so much of what Anne did, it is always made by commentators to trail along in her sisters' wake. It is as if, in addressing it after having tried to analyse the never-easily analysable novels of Charlotte and Emily, the collective critical will had somehow run out of steam. That this should be so is a serious matter. The low estimate of the book has contributed more than any other factor to Anne's unenviable status as a Brontë also-ran.

For the fact is that it is a substantial novel with important and well-worked-out themes. If it falters here and there – notably in the somewhat breathless, and unnecessary, melodrama of the dénouement – it contains, in Helen Huntingdon, one of the strongest and most sympathetic of all Brontë heroines.

In it, Anne Brontë gives the impression of having learnt from the shortcomings of *Agnes Grey,* and of having learnt from Emily, notably in the recapitulatory method she here employs. It is a much more spacious book than *Agnes Grey.* And, given Anne's reputation as a somewhat stern moralist, one of a certain freedom of manners. Thus, the narrator, male protagonist and eventually successful suitor for Helen's hand, Gilbert Markham, is at first allowed a substantial and somewhat unprincipled flirtation with the vicar's youngest daughter, Eliza, before deciding that he really wants to be in love with his mysterious new neighbour. And when the lady does not reciprocate his sudden disposition to be interested in her, we learn, when she offers her hand on the second or third meeting:

> I gave it a spiteful squeeze; for I was annoyed at the injustice
> she had done me from the very dawn of our acquaintance.

It is a rather refreshing spurt of naked jealousy, handled in a delightfully spontaneous manner. And Markham's youthful unscrupulousness where women are concerned is underlined a few pages later in the book when he is to be found with Eliza again, "snatching a kiss behind her father's back, while he was enveloping his throat and chin in the folds of a mighty comforter". It is behaviour more emancipated (between those, that is, who are not yet acknowledged lovers) than is to be found elsewhere in the Brontës' pages. Yet Anne is not censorious about it in the slightest.

Markham's quarrelsomeness as a lover is something with which she is also, quite at home. His jealous assault on Helen's brother Lawrence (in the misapprehension that they are rivals for Helen's love) might so easily have degenerated into Gothic pastiche. But it doesn't. Anne has seen such behaviour from the young men of her native Yorkshire. And in the midst of a passionate exchange which has Markham knocking Lawrence from his horse, her countrywoman's eye never falters.

> The pony, surprised to be so strangely relieved of its burden, started and capered and kicked a little, and then made use of its freedom to go and crop the grass of the hedge bank.

Sex and the handling of it, does not seem to be a problem for Anne. It is a part of Helen's marriage to Huntingdon in a way it never is in Jane Eyre's relationship with Rochester (nor, of course, Cathy's with Heathcliff). We are made to believe in Huntingdon's dissolute past when he tells his bride that the route of their honeymoon Grand Tour will be paved with his ex-mistresses. Beside him, Rochester is a mere posturer. Neither his past nor his present conduct have about them the sickening certainty of sexual betrayal that Huntingdon brings to his marriage. Huntingdon and his cronies are bad men, and they mean to do bad things to their women. Charlotte's problem in *Jane Eyre* (one germane to her masochistic nature) was that she wanted us to admire the 'bad' Rochester, and then to sympathise with his (psychologically unconvincing) redemption.

Anne is more clear sighted. And yet she does not make Helen moralise. One of the great things about this book is that she has painted an entirely convincing portrait of a young woman wanting to believe in, and be in love with, a bad man, without diminishing her dignity. Huntingdon has returned home, shattered in body and mind after a months-long debauch in town.

"What are you crying for, Helen? What the deuce is the matter now?"

"I'm crying for you, Arthur," I replied, speedily drying my tears; and starting up, I threw myself on my knees before him, and, clasping his nerveless hand between my own, continued: "Don't you know that you are a part of myself? And do you think you can injure and degrade yourself and I not feel it?"

Huntingdon is still not beyond redemption. He has the taste to realise he is doing injury to a finely tempered spirit. After a certain amount of shamefaced shuffling he asks her for a restorative glass of wine, which she fetches.

"What a shame it is," said I as I took the empty glass from his hand, "for a strong young man like you to reduce yourself to such a state!"

He replies:

"Ah, if you knew all, my girl, you'd say rather 'What a wonder it is that you bear it so well as you do!' I've lived more in these four months, Helen, than you have in the whole course of your existence ..."

This return of complacency in an erring husband who was, moments before, cringing under his wife's articulate reproaches, but now knows he is well on the road to securing her forgiveness, is acutely observed. Anne is so much more at home with the male psyche than Charlotte is. In a Charlotte novel we cannot imagine sex, on stage, so to speak. Rochester's indiscretions were long ago. All her other male characters are chaste. But Helen is to have her nose rubbed in her husband's adultery. Her rival, Lady Lowborough, is allowed to exult over her, telling her, in effect, that she has only herself to blame, for not making herself a more enticing woman for him. And Huntingdon's other house guests behave only a little less basely than himself. His friend Hargrave tries to seduce her and subjects her to relentless moral blackmail. One of the finest things in the book is the moment of horror Helen feels when she realises that for a brief moment she has felt half-tempted to encourage his advances, merely as a means of recovering some self-esteem.

The cuckolded Lord Lowborough, too, is profoundly unsympathetic. When he learns of his wife's apostasy, his reaction is to heap reproaches on Helen for not having told him earlier. But this is not a doctrinaire attack on men's baseness on Anne's part. We feel powerful indignation, too, that in the middle of almost unendurable mental sufferings, Helen must be assailed by this inadequate peer who has not the courage – as she has – to face what is happening to him. We are made to experience, with her, the nature of woman's helplessness in the man's world she inhabits. And Anne does not inflict on us one word of authorial comment on the subject.

Wildfell Hall is a graphic enactment of the moral disintegration of a man's character, and its power to involve others in its ruin. Huntingdon's attempt to make his own infant son an alcoholic is truly shocking. The drunken and degrading brawling between the dinner guests is portrayed in vivid detail. The callousness with which Huntingdon picks up with the new governess, when his affair with Lady Lowborough has worn itself out, is deeply felt by us on Helen's behalf. At the end, admittedly, the book suffers from a certain loss of focus. In the interests of tying up loose ends, the mechanics of the plot come under strain. As we move to a union between the two lovers after Huntingdon's death, there is a descent into the conventional. Markham must be made to wait for his virtuous widow. As a merely anxious suitor, he seems a radically less interesting character than he did earlier.

Yet if it is not, in the ultimate analysis, so *successful* a novelistic performance as *Jane Eyre* and is not, therefore, read with quite the surface satisfaction Charlotte's romantic melodrama gives, *The Tenant of Wildfell Hall* has moments of equal seriousness and power. Unlike *Jane Eyre* it does not betray psychological truth, and never compromises with itself. It is certainly a better, more fundamentally serious, novel than either *Shirley* or *Villette*.

11 THE BRONTËS AS POETS

THERE has been general agreement about the relative merits of the Brontës as poets. In this consensus Charlotte is negligible, Emily preeminent, Anne effective but minor. Emily was included by Helen Gardner in her *New Oxford Book of English Verse 1250-1950* (1972), where she received a respectable representation of six poems. (Q had failed to notice her in his *Oxford Book of English Verse 1250-1918,* of 1939.) Beyond the general agreement, there is a greater degree of discussion when it comes down to specifics, notably as to the precise stature of Emily. Is she indisputably a major lyric poet, one of the greatest in the language? Is she, rather, merely a substantial *woman* lyric poet? Or is she, even if a diamond of any sort, a pretty rough one?

The claims of Charlotte are easily tested. To be fair to her, she entirely disclaimed any merits as a poet and told Mrs Gaskell she would rather not have her contribution to the *Poems* of 1846 subjected to further scrutiny. Given this, it is surprising to see that she is represented at more than twice the length of her sisters, in that volume. But it seems likely that Emily and Anne were reluctant to disgorge for public consumption the number of poems that would have been required for a volume of the length Charlotte had promised the publisher, and that she had to make up the weight.

As we have already seen from her poetic Valentine to Weightman, she was a ready versifier. This impression is reinforced in her contribution to the *Poems*. She deploys verse as a vehicle for story telling comfortably enough. She never has the difficulties with rhythm and rhyme which are all too frequent in Emily. But her verse is essentially prose, and performs much the same function as prose. Many of her contributions to *Poems* are, in fact, not lyric but lengthy narrative poems, hauled, one senses, unceremoniously out of the pages of the Angria chronicles. When she is asked to distil thought or experience in a lyric her shortcomings are manifest. The sententious "Life"

Life, believe, is not a dream
So dark as sages say;
Oft a little morning rain
Foretells a pleasant day.
Sometimes there are clouds of gloom,
But these are transient all;
If the showers will make the roses bloom,
Oh why lament its fall?
Rapidly, merrily,
Life's sunny hours flit by,
Gratefully, cheerily, Enjoy them as they fly!

is scarcely credible as the utterance of a woman of Charlotte's intelligence, sensitivity and painful experience of life. (It is not one of her juvenilia but written at 23, no great age perhaps, but certain maturity for a shortlived Brontë.)

But there is no need to labour the point. Charlotte Brontë reserved her poetry for her novels, a pity, perhaps, since verse as a means of examining her deepest emotions might have provided the control she is so often not under in prose. Only in her verse reflection on the death of Emily:

My darling you will never know
The grinding agony of woe
That we have borne for thee.

did the sheer immensity of the experience wring from her, for once, a mature poem which is a memorable cry of pain.

As Janet Gezari has pointed out in the introduction to her *Emily Jane Brontë: The Complete Poems* (Penguin, 1992), there are frequent difficulties in determining where an Emily poem was meant to begin or end. Poems originally brought to birth in a Gondal setting were changed by her for inclusion in the *Poems* of 1846, to make them more generally accessible. They might later be reworked by her with other purposes in mind. Other poems, published posthumously, passed through the editing filter of Charlotte to polish their 'rough' edges and render them more tasteful. Even Arthur Bell Nicholls has had his editorial say on what of Emily's output might, or might not, be fit for the consumption of posterity. To this is added the difficulty of transcribing, from notebooks and scraps of paper, poems written in a cramped and microscopic hand. The arrangement of C. W. Hatfield in his edition of 1941 is the one generally agreed upon. But it is, in the nature of the thing, not infallible.

In some editions, as many as three separate poems have been identified from what in others is printed as a single work. Thus, the often-discussed "Julian M. and A. G. Rochelle" has spawned numerous progeny. Its most famous, the often-anthologised "The Visionary" (included by Helen Gardner in her *New Oxford Book*), is actually 40 per cent Charlotte's work. Looking among her sisters' literary remains for some poems to accompany the posthumous 1850 edition of *Wuthering Heights* and *Agnes Grey,* Charlotte espied three promising stanzas among an otherwise rambling poem of Emily's, added two more of her own, and retitled them. A succession of editors and anthologists has accepted the result. But clearly that 'result' gets us no further in assessing Emily's merits as a poet, and should be removed from the canon.

In the *New Oxford Book* the problem is exacerbated by Helen Gardner's having printed immediately after "The Visionary" a poem called "The Prisoner", which is actually another excision from "Julian M. and A. G. Rochelle". This excerpt (often printed but generally acknowledged as being what it is) is, I think, a legitimate one. (Q himself was an adept at selecting from rambling – generally mediaeval – poems.) But the effect can be mischievous when printed, as it is in the *New Oxford Book*, alongside a poem of spurious genesis. To the unwary, two poems of such a character among a representation of only six, proselytise strongly for the view that Emily was 'mystical', a problem we shall address later.

Nevertheless, if we stand on established certainties, there is still plenty by which Emily Brontë can be legitimately judged as a poet. It has to be admitted that she is an extraordinarily patchy performer.

This has something to do with the fact that in the first instance, verse written for private consumption was exhumed and asked to stand duty for something else. Emily chose to publish a novel. She did not choose to become a published poet. That does not mean that Charlotte was wrong to make her one. But there is a good deal of truth in Robin Grove's observation:

> " ... to work through C. W. Hatfield's edition, reading the poems in order, is a disconcerting experience. To be sure, a number of the finest and best-known come where we might expect, near to the end of Brontë's life; but the first lyric in the book is quite as good as most of her writing ten years later, while her last extant piece ... handles its revenge theme – all "taunts and noble gore" – as if she had never read, let alone written, *Wuthering Heights*. What we seem to have is an author who gained access to her talents rarely: from time to time, and apparently at random, wrote poems of real worth ..."

What immediately strikes us from the author of *Wuthering Heights* is that the economy and vividness of description – particularly of scenery, and atmospheric effects – is almost totally lacking the in the poetry. A stock vocabulary: "wild", "desolate", "waste", "dreary", "despair" reigns here. And even in poems where the 'nature' component is intended merely to be at the service of a state of mind, this verbal inertness is fatal to the result.

The night is darkening round me,
The wild winds coldly blow;
But a tyrant spell has bound me
And I cannot, cannot go.

The giant trees are bending
Their bare bows weighed with snow,
And the storm is fast descending
And yet I cannot go.

Clouds beyond clouds above me,
Wastes beyond wastes below;
But nothing drear can move me;
I will not, cannot go.

The poem has been much admired and often anthologised. Even the judicious Grove awards it, so to speak, full marks. I confess I cannot see where its merits lie. This landscape could have come out of Thomson's *Seasons* with its "wild winds", "giant trees" and "bare boughs". (What is Emily doing, anyway, talking about "giant trees" among the stunted hawthorns of her native moors?) Against this amateurish daub of a scenic background, the "tyrant spell" which holds the speaker in thrall becomes yet another stock epithet. We can have no inkling of what psychological or spiritual state it stands for. The apparent complexity of state of mind – the inability to move and the unwillingness to do so even if she could – is not worked out nor even evoked in the poem. The word "drear" lies leadenly on that penultimate line. The refrain becomes merely banal.

The best of the Emily Brontë poems are those where nature and its ramifications have no part, where we are, instead, exposed to the unvarnished workings of that autonomous mind and iron will. The most famous (if not necessarily the most attractive) of these is the late "No coward soul is mine". I say not necessarily the most attractive, not merely because we instinctively shrink from the apparent arrogance of the third stanza (it is more apparent than real, the poet means not that these creeds are intrinsically worthless but that they will not shake her faith):

Vain are the thousand creeds
That move men's hearts, unutterably vain,
Worthless as withered weeds
Or idlest froth amid the boundless main

but because the stanza which expresses this is also the weakest in the poem. The last line of it is an ill-thought out and badly expressed schoolgirl simile which drags the poem down dreadfully. Nevertheless, the second-stanza invocation to the "God within my breast" is *echte* Emily. And it carries us to the assertion of the final one with irresistible compulsion.

> There is not room for death
> Nor atom that his might could render void
> Since thou art Being and Breath
> And what thou art may never be destroyed.

Which is a convenient point at which to examine claims for Emily's having a mystic vision. Before we go any further let us be quite sure what we mean by mystical. We do not mean misty; we do not mean the imagining of spiritual forces in natural forms, such as we get in Wordsworth; we mean direct apprehension of God and spiritual reality without intermediary assistance from an established religion (though it may require severely disciplined meditation).

Now this state is *approached* by Emily on occasions. In "I'm happiest when most away" she celebrates the flight of her soul from the confines of the body. But union with the divine does not seem to be the object of that escape: rather, "spirit wandering wide/ Through infinite immensity." And as we have already seen, the 'mysticism' of "The Visionary" is a thing restrospectively synthesised by Charlotte. When read closely it can be seen for what it is: a jumble of bogus sentiment. Perhaps the nearest thing we have in Emily Brontë to the description of a trance-like mystical state occurs in that section of "Julian M. and A.G. Rochelle" which she herself chose to publish as an entity in the 1846 *Poems* under the title "The Prisoner" (she chose lines which overlap and include those printed under the same title by Helen Gardner in the *New Oxford Book*).

> But first a hush of peace – a soundless calm descends
> The struggle of distress, and fierce impatience ends;
> Mute music soothes my breast – unuttered harmony,
> That I could never dream, till Earth was lost to me.

Then dawns the Invisible; the Unseen its truth reveals;
My outward sense is gone, my inwards essence feels:
Its wings are almost free – its home its harbour found,
Measuring the gulf, it stoops and dares the final bound.

The clue is in "almost". In the next stanza:

Oh! dreadful is the check – intense the agony –
When the ear begins to hear, and the eye begins to see;

It is clear that this does not, as has been suggested, represent the
pain of return to physical reality after a mystical vision, but the inability
of the spirit to achieve that end (even if it would). In fact, Emily
never does seem to have the intense yearning for union with the divine
which characterises the poetry of the mystic. In "O! thy bright eyes
must answer now", another poem frequently coerced into the mystical
canon on her behalf, she makes it clear – heretical though she knows
it is – that her own inner vision is enough to sustain her.

And am I wrong to worship where
Faith cannot doubt, nor Hope despair,
Since my own soul can grant my prayer?

In her most convincing 'religious' poetry, Emily likes, in fact, to be
her own god, and lay down her own laws.

Finally, the technical accomplishment of Emily Brontë as a poet
has been a matter of some debate. In her essay *A Baby God* Rosalind
Miles salutes the "astonishing confidence" of her style. Yet, as we
have seen, her poetic vocabulary is quite capable of deadening the
reader's desire to follow her, with stock epithets. Her grasp of rhyme
is generally sound, but her ear for rhythm seems often so faulty as to
give the impression she has simply not got down to the study of a few
good models of the art. Rosalind Miles's assertion that her frequent
veerings between different metrical schemes are proof of her ability
to "change gear" within a poem to create "extraordinary daring and
complex" effects, will not, it seems to me, hold water.

> On a sunny brac alone I lay
> One summer afternoon
> It was the marriage time of May
> With her young lover, June.

This may not be great poetry, but it has the unforced simplicity of mediaeval ballad. It is in the tradition of

> In somer when the shawes be sheyne
> And leves be large and long
> Hit is full merye in feyre foreste
> To here the foulys song.

But having got off to such an enchanting start, the rhythm of the poem immediately begins to go wrong.

> From her mother's heart seemed loath to part
> That queen of bridal charms;
> But her father smiled on the fairest child
> He ever held in his arms.

This is already becoming a mess, metrically speaking, with three new rhythms introduced in four lines. What Emily does not seem to realise that in lyric poetry, especially short-lined lyric poetry, form *is* meaning. And her reckless disregard of the former, almost always militates against the latter. It is seen at its most disastrous in

> Come, the wind may never again
> Blow as now it blows for us
> And the stars may never again shine as now they shine;
> Long before October returns,
> Seas of blood will have parted us;
> And you must crush the love in your heart, and I the love in mine!

which is impossible to speak aloud without having the poverty of what is on offer literally forced down one's throat. This metrical indecision – metrical chaos even – affects many of those poems which are regarded as her finest efforts. "Remembrance" is characteristic.

Cold in the earth – and the deep snow piled above thee,
Far, far removed, cold in the dreary grave!
Have I forgot, my only Love, to love thee,
Severed at last by Time's all-severing wave?

This cascade of dactyls, trochees and spondees does not make for successful poetry in English. The emasculating repetitions "Cold in the earth", "cold in the dreary grave"; "far, far removed"; "Severed", "all-severing"; are symptomatic of the desperate shifts to which Emily has to resort, to pad out the unsatisfactory metrical scheme she has got herself into. There *is* a rhythm, but it is a rhythm alien to the natural sinew of the English tongue. It ensures that "Remembrance" remains irritatingly undistinguished and, ironically, unmemorable as a poem, coming from someone so manifestly capable of expressing deep feeling as Emily was.

The inescapable conclusion to be drawn from all this is that as a poet Emily Brontë actually functions some way below the level of the more reckless claims that have been made on her behalf. She is capable of moments of power, but they are remarkably few and far between. There seems no link between the imagination and sheer craft that produced *Wuthering Heights* and the go-as-you-please feeling that lies behind her poetry. The novel solidly inhabits the world of reality and makes literature of it, in a way the poems rarely do. Gondal – and the degree of immaturity which is inseparable from the continuing to dabble in such an exercise – haunts the poetry until the end of Emily's productive life. But neither it, nor its characters, ever seem to touch, or have any part of, the creative source which gave rise to *Wuthering Heights*.

Anne Brontë's performance as a poet is in marked contrast. There is a clear transition from the Gondal juvenilia to the philosophical poems of her maturity. More important, her Christianity, which in the novels was under creative control, is the guiding principle here. That is not to disparage her achievement on those grounds. Anne Brontë is a religious poet in a way Emily, and certainly Charlotte, are not. Her writing was influenced by William Cowper, whom all the sisters admired, and by the stream of 18th century evangelical hymn writing. She herself wrote hymns, a handful of which are represented in *The Methodist Hymn Book* as well as other Nonconformist collections.

Unlike Emily, Anne is not a Romantic. Her natural dwelling place (as a poet, not of course as novelist) is the 18th century. And, again, unlike Emily, she continually strove to perfect her verse technique. Her revision of her homage to William Cowper demonstrates the point. The first version, written in 1842, opens:

> Sweet are thy strains Celestial Bard
> And oft in early childhood's years
> I've read them o'er and o'er again
> With swelling heart and gushing tears.

Its successor:

> Sweet are thy strains, Celestial Bard,
> And oft in childhood's years
> I've read them o'er and o'er again
> With floods of silent tears.

The gain, in the succinctness of the thing, is immediately apparent from the shortening of the *b* and *d* lines of the quatrain to three stresses. In the course of it, the redundant "early" in line 2 and the lushly-clichéd "swelling" and "gushing" of line 4 have been eliminated. But the gain is not merely a matter of effectiveness but of sincerity. It is a quietly impressive determination from the poet to extract as much as possible from the (admittedly limited) materials at her disposal.

Anne Brontë uses her religious poems to wrestle out her beliefs and doubts over contemporaneous doctrinal issues as none of her sisters do. Her celebrated attack on the Calvinist doctrine of election bursts from her with an indignation that is nevertheless well under control. And her switch of form from the iambic pentameters with which she delivers the polemic part of the poem:

> You may rejoice to think yourselves secure,
> You may be grateful for the gift divine
> That grace unsought which made your black hearts pure
> And fits your earthborn souls in Heaven to shine.

to the common metre of hymn with which she asserts her own belief in salvation:

> And O! there lives within my heart
> A hope long nursed by me...

is a nicely calculated one.
In her hymns she is not always in such a consoling mood.

> Believe not those who say
> The upward path is smooth
> Lest thou should stumble in the way
> And faint before the truth.

promises Bunyanesque tribulation before the goal is reached. As Edward Chitham has remarked, many of these hymns are too introspective to be effective in communal worship. And, as can be seen, as hymnal fare they rate some way below the productions of Cowper or Isaac Watts.

In her personal poems – particularly poems of personal loss – we encounter a somewhat different persona, one more susceptible to Romantic influences. The emotionalism of the following is often ascribed to her remembered love for the long-dead Weightman.

> Severed and gone, so many years!
> And art thou still so dear to me,
> That throbbing heart and burning tears
> Can witness how I clung to thee.

> I know that in the narrow tomb
> The form I loved was buried deep,

And left, in silence and in gloom,
To slumber out its dreamless sleep.

I know the corner where it lies
Is but a weary place of rest:
The charnel moisture never dries
From the dark flagstones o'er its breast.

This comes perilously close to the sobbing manner of the Gondal juvenilia. Stanza three may be an accurate description of the corner of Haworth churchyard in which Weightman lies. But it does not acquit the poem of a descent into the Gothic with its "charnel moisture" and "dark flagstones" o'er the breast. Yet later in the same poem Anne Brontë casts this morbidity aside and emerges onto the plane of

Life seems more sweet that thou didst live,
And men more true that thou wert one:
Nothing is lost that thou didst give,
Nothing destroyed that thou hast done.

This is still emotional. But the emotion is under a control that enables it to function as something more than personal grief. In the opening of the poem the late lamented is merely a rotting corpse. In this quatrain he is seen *sub specie aeternitatis* as a human being.

* * * *

In conclusion, the poems do not really add to the literary stature of the Brontës. On a rereading, Charlotte remains negligible; Emily is too slipshod a technician to do justice to her soaring imagination; Anne has her, generally religious, thoughts under too strict a curb to achieve the naked indignation, pity and power to move, which inform her novels. The verdict must be that had not the novels followed, the Brontë sisters must have remained unknown, or at least obscure. Yet the irony is that it was the *Poems,* the least considerable portion of their *oeuvre,* that gave impetus to their greatest efforts, and that it was Charlotte, the least considerable performer in that volume, who was the source of that impetus.

And it has to be admitted that whatever we say about the dangers of reading from the sisters' lives into their works, those lives do have a fascination in themselves. In spite of all that rational enquiry and research can do, the daily round at Haworth Parsonage has, for better or for worse, assumed a fictional dimension in the imaginations of succeeding generations – and will never really lose it. There is a heroic quality in the sheer endeavour against the odds of obscurity and timidity and, when those were overcome, disease, which seems to elevate the Brontë story itself to the level of art.

We cannot know whether the sisters would have produced much more of value than they did, had they lived. The evidence is that Charlotte had quarried her imagination of all it had to deliver. In Emily's case, it is simply difficult to imagine a successor to *Wuthering Heights.* Anne gave indications that she was learning her craft as a novelist. But her religious faith was always a threat to her creative imagination, and might have marred any later fiction, as it did not her poetry.

We have to be content with what we have: and that is that in *Wuthering Heights* we have a work of passionate intensity which is unique among European novels; that in *Jane Eyre,* flawed, even reprehensible, though its psychology is, we have a romantic melodrama that will, somehow, never wear out its popular appeal; and that in *Wildfell Hall* we have a startling account of the cruelty a man can wantonly inflict on a woman trapped in marriage to him, which is valid for any age.

As contemporary reaction to them shows, all three novels broke the bounds of what was acceptable in fiction. That they created no tradition does not matter. They scarcely could have done, springing from the strange soil they did. Their authors' lack of experience sometimes gave rise to excrescences of thought and emotion which were not fully worked out even by themselves. But they repositioned the frontiers of realism in the English novel, and placed woman and her insurgent desires at the centre of the stage. It was a position from which, for their successors, there was to be no going back.

FURTHER READING

Critical and biographical studies

The Life of Charlotte Brontë by Elizabeth Gaskell (1857). The first in the field, and still indispensable for an understanding of the Brontë ethos.

Haworth Parsonage A Picture of the Brontë Family by Isabel C. Clarke (1927). Biased and impassioned. Often short on (and impatient of) fact, but undeniably stimulating.

Anne Brontë by Winifred Gerin (1959). Like her later biography of Emily, a strangely patchy book, with a good deal of the bland and commonplace interspersed, nevertheless, with moments of genuine insight.

Wuthering Heights An Anthology of Criticism compiled by Alastair Everitt (1967). Viewpoints from both British and American critics over the past hundred years. Has no particular axe to grind and is refreshingly unacademic.

The Art of Emily Brontë ed. Anne Smith (1976). A variety of more or less recent viewpoints on *Wuthering Heights* and the poetry.

The Madwoman in the Attic: The Woman Writer and the Nineteenth Century Imagination by Sandra Gilbert and Susan Gubar (1979). Generally regarded as being the key feminist critique, it is far less stimulating than the promise held out in the title.

Everyman's Companion to the Brontës by Barbara and Gareth Lloyd Evans (1982). At first glance merely a handy crib, this in fact contains many sound judgements and acute insights, as well as being an intelligently compiled reference work.

Critical Essays on Charlotte Brontë ed. Barbara Timm Gates (1990). Useful collection which airs a wide range of views, from G. H. Lewes and Mrs Humphrey Ward to the latest feminist thinking.

A Chainless Soul: A Life of Emily Brontë by K. Frank (1990). Like most 'biographies' of Emily it relies on accumulated speculation to make its effect.

The Brontës by Juliet Barker (1994). Compendious and exhaustively researched. But in seeking to demonstrate that the Brontë sisters were 'normal' and that there was nothing mysterious about the sources of their creativity, Mrs Barker comes close to throwing the baby out with the bathwater. There is a somewhat perverse emphasis on Branwell's contribution.

Emily Brontë: Heretic by Stevie Davis (1994). Has moments of insight but is generally ruined by doctrinaire feminism and an insistence on imposing the standards of the latter 20th century on the Brontë world.

The Brontës: A Life in Letters ed. Juliet Barker (1997). In letting the Brontës and their correspondents tell the story themselves this actually makes for a more compelling evocation of the sisters' lives than Juliet Barker's much longer biography does.

GREENWICH EXCHANGE BOOKS

Student Guides

Greenwich Exchange Student Guides are critical studies of major or contemporary serious writers in English and selected European languages. The series is for the Student, the Teacher and the 'common reader' and are ideal resources for libraries. The *Times Educational Supplement (TES)* praised these books saying "The style of these guides has a pressure of meaning behind it. Students should learn from that ... If art is about selection, perception and taste, then this is it."

(ISBN prefix 1-871551- applies).
The series includes:
W. H. Auden by Stephen Wade (-36-6)
William Blake by Peter Davies (-27-7)
The Brontës by Peter Davies (-24-2)
Joseph Conrad by Martin Seymour-Smith (-18-8)
William Cowper by Michael Thorn (-25-0)
Charles Dickens by Robert Giddings (-26-9)
John Donne by Sean Haldane (-23-4)
Thomas Hardy by Sean Haldane (-35-1)
Philip Larkin by Warren Hope (-35-8)
Shakespeare's Poetry by Martin Seymour-Smith (-22-6)
Tobias Smollett by Robert Giddings (-21-8)
Alfred Lord Tennyson by Michael Thorn (-20-X)
William Wordsworth by Andrew Keanie (57-9)
W.B. Yeats by Warren Hope (-34-X)

Other titles planned include:
20th Century: T. S. Eliot; Ford Madox Ford; Robert Graves; Dylan Thomas
19th Century: Arnold; Jane Austen; Browning; Byron; John Clare; S. T. Coleridge; George Eliot; John Keats; Oscar Wilde;
18th Century: Fielding, Dr Johnson; Alexander Pope; Richardson; Laurence Sterne; Sheridan; Dean Swift
17th Century: Congreve; Dryden; Ben Jonson; Marlowe; Milton; Rochester

Early writings: Chaucer; Skelton

European Languages
Fifty European Novels by Martin Seymour-Smith (-49-8)

French Authors
Balzac by Wendy Mercer (-48-X)

Other titles planned include:
Apollinaire; Céline; Gide; Proust; Rimbaud; Tournier, Verlaine; Zola

German Authors
Goethe; Heine; Thomas Mann; Rilke

132

OTHER GREENWICH EXCHANGE BOOKS

All paperbacks unless otherwise stated.

LITERATURE & BIOGRAPHY

"The Author, the Book & the Reader" *by Robert Giddings*
This collection of Essays analyses the effects of changing technology and the attendant commercial pressures on literary styles and subject matter. Authors covered include Dickens; Smollett; Mark Twain; Dr Johnson; John Le Carré.
ISBN 1-871551-01-0; A5 size; 220pp; illus.

"In Pursuit of Lewis Carroll" *by Raphael Shaberman*
Sherlock Holmes and the author uncover new evidence in their investigations into the mysterious life and writing of Lewis Carroll. They examine published works by Carroll that have been overlooked by previous commentators. A newly discovered poem, almost certainly by Carroll, is published here. Amongst many aspects of Carroll's highly complex personality, this book explores his relationship with his parents, numerous child friends, and the formidable Mrs Liddell, mother of the immortal Alice.
ISBN 1-871551-13-7; 70% A4 size; 130pp; illus.

"Norman Cameron" *by Warren Hope*
Cameron's poetry was admired by Auden; celebrated by Dylan Thomas; valued by Robert Graves. He was described by Martin Seymour-Smith as one of "... the most rewarding and pure poets of his generation..." and is at last given a full length biography. This eminently sociable man, who had periods of darkness and despair, wrote little poetry by comparison with others of his time, but always of a high and consistent quality - imaginative and profound.
ISBN 1-871551-05-6; A5 size; 250pp; illus.

"Liar! Liar!": Jack Kerouac–Novelist" *by R. J. Ellis*
The fullest study of Jack Kerouac's fiction to date. It is the first book to devote an individual chapter to each and every one of his novels. *On the Road, Visions of Cody* and *The Subterraneans*, Kerouac's central masterpieces, are re-read in-depth, in a new and exciting way. The books Kerouac himself saw as major elements of his spontaneous 'bop' odyssey, *Visions of Gerard* and *Doctor Sax*, are also strikingly reinterpreted, as are other, daringly innovative writings, like 'The Railroad Earth' and his 'try at a spontaneous *Finnegans Wake*', *Old Angel Midnight*. Undeservedly neglected writings, such as *Tristessa* and *Big Sur*, are also analysed, alongside better known novels like *Dharma Bums* and *Desolation Angels*.
Liar! Liar! takes its title for the words of *Tristessa's* narrator, Jack, referring to himself. He also warns us 'I guess, I'm a liar, watch out!'. R. J. Ellis' study provocatively proposes that we need to take this warning seriously and, rather than reading Kerouac's novels simply as fictional versions of his life, focus just as much on the way the novels stand as variations on a series of ambiguously-represented themes:

133

explorations of class, sexual identity, the French-Canadian Catholic confessional, and addiction in its hydra-headed modern forms. Ellis shows how Kerouac's deep anxieties in each of these arenas makes him an incisive commentator on his uncertain times and a bitingly honest self-critic, constantly attacking his narrators' 'vanities'. R. J. Ellis is Professor of English and American Studies at the Nottingham Trent University. His commentaries on Beat writing have been frequently published, and his most recent book, a full modern edition of Harriet Wilson's *Our Nig*, the first ever novel by an African American woman, has been widely acclaimed.
ISBN 1-871551-53-6; A5 size; 300pp

PHILOSOPHY

"Marx: Justice and Dialectic" *by James Daly*
Department of Scholastic Philosophy, Queen's University, Belfast.
James Daly shows the humane basis of Marx's thinking, rather than the imposed "economic materialistic" views of many modem commentators. In particular he refutes the notion that for Marx, justice relates simply to the state of development of society at a particular time. Marx's views about justice and human relationships belong to the continuing traditions of moral thought in Europe.
ISBN 1-871551-28-5; A5 size; 180 pp

"Questions of Platonism" *by Ian Leask*
In a daring challenge to contemporary orthodoxy, Ian Leask subverts both Hegel and Heidegger by arguing for a radical re-evaluation of Platonism. Thus, while he traces a profoundly Platonic continuity between ancient Athens and 19th century Germany, the nature of this Platonism, he suggests, is neither 'totalizing' nor Hegelian but, instead, open-ended 'incomplete' and oriented towards a divine goal beyond *logos* or any metaphysical structure. Such a re-evaluation exposes the deep anti-Platonism of Hegel's absolutizing of volitional subjectivity; it also confirms Schelling as true modern heir to the 'constitutive incompletion' of Plato and Plotinus.By providing a more nuanced approach - refusing to accept either Hegel's self-serving account of 'Platonism' or the (equally totalizing) post-Heideggerian inversion of this narrative – Leask demonstrates the continued relevance of a genuine, 'finite' Platonic quest. Ian Leask teaches in the Department of Scholastic Philosophy at the Queen's University of Belfast.
ISBN 1-871551-32-3; A5 size; 154pp

"The Philosophy of Whitehead" *by Dr T. E. Burke*
Department of Philosophy, University of Reading
Dr Burke explores the main achievements of this philosopher, better known in the US than Britain. Whitehead, often remembered as Russell's tutor and collaborator on *Principia Mathematica,* was one of the few who had a grasp of relativity and its possible implications. His philosophical writings reflect his profound knowledge of mathematics and science. He was responsible for initiating process theology.
ISBN 1-871551-29-3; A5 size; 106pp

POETRY

"Lines from the Stone Age" *by Sean Haldane*
Reviewing Sean Haldane's 1992 volume *Desire in Belfast* Robert Nye wrote in The *Times* that 'Haldane can be sure of his place among the English poets.' The facts that his early volumes appeared in Canada and that he has earned his living by other means than literature have meant that this place is not yet a conspicuous one, although his poems have always had their circle of readers. The 60 previously unpublished poems of *Lines from the Stone Age* – 'lines of longing, terror, pride, lust and pain' – may widen this circle.
ISBN 1-871551-39-0; A5 size; 58pp

"Wilderness" *by Martin Seymour-Smith*
This is Seymour-Smith's first publication of his poetry for more than 20 years. This collection of 36 poems is a fearless account of an inner life of love, frustration, guilt, laughter and the celebration of others. Best known to the general public as the author of the controversial and best selling *Hardy* (1994).
ISBN 1-871551-08-0; A5 size; 64pp

Baudelaire: "Les Fleurs du Mal in English Verse" *translated by Professor F. W. Leakey*
Selected poems from *Les Fleurs du Mal* are translated with parallel French texts, are designed to be read with pleasure by readers who have no French, as well as those practised in the French language.
F. W. Leakey is Emeritus Professor of French in the University of London. As a scholar, critic and teacher he has specialised in the work of Baudelaire for 50 years. He has published a number of books on Baudelaire.
ISBN 1-871551-10-2; A5 size; 140pp

"Shakespeare's Sonnets" *edited by Martin Seymour-Smith*
This scholarly edition follows the original text of the 1609 Quarto - which, with newly revised notes and introduction by Seymour-Smith – provides an insight with which to judge Shakespeare's artistic intentions.
ISBN 1-871551-38-2; A5 size; 120pp

"Shakespeare's Non-Dramatic Poetry" *by Martin Seymour-Smith*
In this study, completed shortly before his death in 1998, Martin Seymour-Smith sheds fresh light on two very different groups of Shakespeare's non-dramatic poems: the early and conventional *Venus and Adonis* and *The Rape of Lucrece*, and the highly personal *Sonnets*. He explains the genesis of the first two in the genre of Ovidian narrative poetry
in which a young Elizabethan man of letters was expected to excel, and which was highly popular. In the *Sonnets* (his 1963 old-spelling edition of which is being reissued by Greenwich Exchange) he traces the mental journey of a man going through an acute psychological crisis as he faces up to the truth about his own unconventional sexuality.

It is a study which confronts those "disagreeables" in the *Sonnets* which most critics have ignored.
ISBN 1-871551-22-6; A5 size; 90pp

FICTION

"The Case of the Scarlet Woman - Sherlock Holmes and the Occult" *by Watkin Jones*
A haunted house, a mysterious kidnapping and a poet's demonic visions are just the beginnings of three connected cases that lead Sherlock Holmes into confrontation with the infamous black magician Aleister Crowley and, more sinisterly, his scorned Scarlet Woman.
The fact that Dr Watson did not publish details of these investigations is perhaps testament to the unspoken fear he and Homes harboured for the supernatural. *The Case of the Scarlet Woman* convinced them both that some things cannot be explained by cold logic.
ISBN 1-871551-14-5; A5 size; 130pp

THEATRE

"Music Hall Warriors: A history of the Variety Artistes Federation" *by Peter Honri*
This is an unique and fascinating history of how vaudeville artistes formed the first effective actor's trade union in 1906 and then battled with the powerful owners of music halls to obtain fairer contracts. The story continues with the VAF dealing with performing rights, radio, and the advent of television. Peter Honri is the fourth generation of a vaudeville family. The book has a foreword by the Right Honourable John Major MP when he was Prime Minister – his father was a founder member of the VAF.
ISBN 1-871551-06-4; A4 size; 140pp; illus.

MISCELLANEOUS

"The Essential Accounting Dictionary of Key Financial Terms" *by Linda Jane Hodgson*
A key aide for students seeking examination success in Accounting A-Level and GNVQ Advanced Business. It results from work with teachers and students and addresses common difficulties. The definitions are straightforward , easy to read, and form the basis of understanding and better performance at tests and examinations. There is a multi-choice quiz to crosscheck how much the student knows.
Linda Jane Hodgson, is a graduate in History and Politics, a former Tax Inspector and a qualified teacher. Professionally, she has also advised accounting firms on taxation. She now teaches business and finance at a London college and organises business and industry links. She is a qualified Young Enterprise Link Teacher.
ISBN 1-871551-50-1; A5 size; 62pp.

"Musical Offering" *by Yolanthe Leigh*
In a series of vivid sketches, anecdotes and reflections, Yolanthe Leigh tells the story of her growing up in the Poland of the nineteen thirties and the second world war. These are poignant episodes of a child's first encounters with both the enchantments and the cruelties of the world; and from a later time, stark memories of the brutality of the Nazi invasion, and the hardships of student life in Warsaw under the Occupation. But most of all this is a record of inward development; passages of remarkable intensity and simplicity describe the girl's response to religion, to music, and to her discovery of philosophy.
The outcome is something unique, a book that eludes classification. In its own distinctive fashion, it creates a memorable picture of a highly perceptive and sensitive individual, set against a background of national tragedy.
ISBN 1-871551-46-3; A5 size 61pp

SHOESTRING PRESS BOOKS

"Raising Spirits, Making Gold & Swapping Wives: The True Adventures of Dr John Dee & Sir Edward Kelly" *by Michael Wilding*
In London in 1583 the mathematician John Dee and the seer Edward Kelly began summoning up a succession of spirits, who instructed them in the secrets of the universe and warned them of imminent apocalyptic change. Attaching themselves to the visiting Polish Count Laski, they set off for Europe, taking with them a mysterious alchemical elixir discovered in the Cotswolds. Queen Elizabeth summoned them back to England to share their alchemical expertise and sent the poet Edward Dyer to collect them.
The surviving confidential reports, letters, diaries and secret spiritual records are assembled there into a compelling narrative, all the more amazing for being truer than any fiction.
Michael Wilding is one of Australia's most distinguished writers. *The New York Times Book Review* said of him, "He's so good that you're willing to forgive him anything." He has published numerous novels and collections of short stories as well as studies of Milton, on whom he is an acknowledged expert, and such ground-breaking critical works as *Social Vision* and *Studies in Classic Australian Fiction*.
ISBN 1-899579-31-5

"Goodbye Buenos Aires" *by Andrew Graham-Yooll*
Buenos Aires in the 1920s and 1930s was a fascinating destination for a young person looking for a new life, a place of fantasy, adventure and prospects of fast wealth. This is the city which the author's father discovered for himself in October, 1928, when he arrived there, penniless from Edinburgh.
This book is at once a memoire of separation, of the harsh reality of unpredictable politics of personal loss, and of love rediscovered.
Andrew Graham-Yooll, who was born in Buenos Aires in 1944, is a journalist on the *Buenos Aires Herald*. He formerly worked for *The Daily Telegraph*, and was the

137

editor of *Index on Censorship*. Among his many books are *A State of Fear*, and *The Forgotten Colony: A History of the English-speaking People in Argentina*.
ISBN 1-899549-36-6